Praise for *Guerrilla Tea*

Jonathan Lear is the voice of the true expert – the excellent classroom teacher who, through experience and experimentation, knows what works for his pupils and is not prepared to let outside interference get in the way of doing what he knows is right for their education and wellbeing. There is a blueprint here for great teaching, but it's not one the author would have readers follow. Instead, in analysing his methods, Jonathan strips away the unnecessary baggage that has begun to clutter the job of teaching, helping professionals recall a time when they felt confident to trust in their own judgement. He is a champion of creativity in the classroom and shares his playful toolkit with readers. And while his penchant for costumes and characters won't be for everyone, the more theatrical elements never come before, or at the expense of, the focus on content and skills. Behind every comedy moustache is the face of real learning – clear objectives, searching questions, and a hard-won understanding of children's development.

Joe Carter, Editor, *Teach Primary*

As educators, we have to stop waiting for a knight in shining armour to come riding over the hill and lead us to our children's promised land. It is up to us – passionate, professional, creative people – to take the lead and revolutionise schooling. Jonathan Lear's authentic and infectious book hits the spot. Use it in order to build your own confidence and capacity and then to lead change for your children in your school!

Richard Gerver, speaker, author, broadcaster

This is a book full of passion. In it Jonathan Lear shares that passion with readers on every page, alongside his wealth of personal experiences in teaching. He skilfully captures a depth of research and communicates this with clarity and ease, and writes with confidence and authority. He talks of starting a revolution with this book and I feel he may just do that. Full of great ideas to take immediately into the classroom and a philosophy that is refreshing and forward thinking. A great read for the next generation of teachers!

Dr Jonathan Doherty, Head of Primary Education,
Leeds Trinity University

This is a book about real teaching by a real teacher who has had to work out how to build learning into a school system that should take learning for granted. Jonathan cuts through the rhetoric of the contemporary standards debate with a conversation about how to switch on pupils' learning by being the sort of good teacher they need rather than the deliverer of conventional practice. There are numerous examples of how to make things happen for the good of learning and plenty of tips and suggestions to enable the committed teacher to make progress that they value rather than measure.

People often talk about 'being brave' in schools these days. What is there to be brave about in inspiring pupils to learn? Teaching should be a joy and a constant source of fulfilment. Anyone who engages with this book will find it goes under the barbed wire of current orthodoxies, throws a few grenades at the mythologies of teaching and comes up in the middle of the great learning debate. There are moments of subterfuge and examples of camouflaged teaching and there is the wonderful escape to teaching that is gripping and enjoyable – for pupils and teachers alike.

Engage with this book ... and be a learning guerrilla.

Mick Waters, Professor of Education, Wolverhampton University

This is a book you will enjoy reading. It's full of humour; stories about teaching, stories about students, and jokes. There are plenty of great ideas about teaching and learning too.

It takes real talent to write breezily for 200 pages, and Jonathan Lear manages it without becoming cloying and facile. This is a book with quality and substance behind the humour.

Lear's central metaphor is the guerrilla teacher, not the hairy kind who eat bananas – although there are plenty of these – but the kind who stir things up, go against authority and make things happen.

Being a guerrilla teacher doesn't sound like an easy option in these days of Morganite-micromanagement and I can't see this book being bought on mass for the staff of Ark'ham Academy, but for the rest of us, hiding in the jungle, it's a valuable manual to keep tucked in our rucksacks.

Tim Taylor, Teacher

Jonathan's manifesto is an excellent guide to teaching creatively in the classroom. Jonathan's book stands on the shoulders of the great creative educationalists and encourages a generation of teachers to join the guerrilla revolution. Most manifestos are full of broken promises, *Guerrilla Teaching* delivers an eclectic range of creative teaching 'policies' designed to turn the mere mortal educator into an inspiring guerrilla teacher.

An indispensable book for any teacher wanting to explore their creative pedagogy and inspire their students. *Guerrilla Teaching* is an inspiring call to arms; Jonathan writes with humour and his book persuades us all to join his creative classroom revolution. Anybody who reads Jonathan's book will want to climb the tallest mountain, raise their arms aloft and shout 'I am a guerrilla teacher!'

A fabulous read, Jonathan's guerrilla manifesto takes apart existing teaching methods and rebuilds them, creatively, from scratch. The book contains everything you need to start your very own classroom revolution. I implore every teacher to read *Guerrilla Teaching*: it can only benefit those who really matter – your students, and their futures.

Julian S. Wood, Deputy Head Teacher,
Wybourn Community Primary School

Guerrilla Teaching is a great, practical and inspirational book for any teacher at any point in their career.

It's refreshing to find a book that offers support and advice that will actually make a difference to the way the children we teach learn and enjoy school. It's a book that reminds us to consider the type of people we want our children to grow up to be and how to help them achieve that.

It reminded me why I choose teaching as a career.

Emma Stevenson, Senior Learning Support Teacher,
Fir Vale Family of Schools

Jonathan Lear

GUERRILLA TEACHING

Revolutionary tactics for teachers on the ground, in real classrooms,
working with real children, trying to make a real difference

Independent Thinking Press

First published by

Independent Thinking Press
Crown Buildings, Bancyfelin, Carmarthen, Wales, SA33 5ND, UK
www.independentthinkingpress.com

Independent Thinking Press is an imprint of Crown House Publishing Ltd.

First published 2015.

British Library Cataloguing-in-Publication Data
A catalogue entry for this book is available
from the British Library.

Print ISBN 978-1-78135-232-8
Mobi ISBN 978-1-78135-233-5
ePub ISBN 978-1-78135-234-2
ePDF ISBN 978-1-78135-235-9

Printed and bound in the UK by
Bell & Bain Ltd, Thornliebank, Glasgow

For my incredible (and tolerant) wife Emma and my beautiful daughters Eve and Imogen. I couldn't have done any of this without your love, support and inspiration. Thank you for everything.

xxx

TOSCANINI AND THE LOW-BUDGET MOVIE

A Foreword by Will Ryan

'You can't just walk into a high school [...] and lecture; you'd lose the students. You have to dance with them, be a drill sergeant, priest, minister, shoulder to cry on and housekeeper. Like Toscanini and a master psychologist rolled into one.' These are the words of Frank McCourt in an interview with the *TES*. The question is where might you go to find such a learning environment? If you want to know more then read on.

I remember my first visit to Jonathan Lear's classroom. I really didn't want to go at first. Now don't get me wrong, I love visiting classrooms and I have been lucky enough to visit some of the best primary classrooms in this nation. However I had squeezed this visit into a tight and hectic schedule and I had arrived at a school that I didn't really know, gone straight into the classroom and found myself in the company of a man who, on first impression, seemed slightly mad. However the wide-opened eyes of the youngsters, who were hanging on to his every word, told me there certainly wasn't any kind of safeguarding issue in the insanity which was about to unfold. What I was really witnessing was a hugely talented practitioner taking children on a magical mystery tour and teaching ten-year-old children as though they were students from an undergraduate course. By the end I found myself not wanting to leave.

In the recent annual reports of Her Majesty's Chief Inspector of Schools we have been told that the quality of teaching continues to rise and is now at the highest level ever. After 42 years in primary education I am convinced that this is correct. However, too often something is missing. Just after the dawn of the twenty-first century Arrowsmith commented, 'the focus on systems, inputs, outputs, data and teacher accountability has been relentless during my eleven years as a head. I struggle to recall a piece of legislation which, when implemented, would have increased children's enjoyment of education and made them want to come to school a little bit more.' He is right. The truth is, in too many classrooms we have learned to teach to a formula where differentiated learning objectives are declared, children sit glued to interactive whiteboards and three-part lessons are interspersed with short term 'teach and do' activities, followed by plenaries and mini-plenaries. Then we go on to a new set of objectives in the next lesson. In short we have become brilliant at the science of pedagogy. This kind of methodology has become accepted as being what inspectors want, and so that is what we provide. It has raised the floor in terms of improving teaching quality, however; it has not raised the ceiling. But fear not, because this book can help!

While there is a science to pedagogy there is also a great art to teaching and this was what I was witnessing in that Year 6 classroom in inner-city Sheffield.

Through his own research Jonathan Lear knows precisely how the brain of a primary aged pupil works. He knows that a balance has to be struck between direct teaching and more exploratory methods. He knows when to support and intervene and when to step back. He understands that children get just one childhood and that enjoyment should be the birthright of every child. He also recognises that childhood in a deprived community, like the one he works in, could be relatively short for some youngsters. In his classroom, and throughout this book, childhood is celebrated and playfulness is accepted.

When Michael Gove was secretary of state for education he removed the picture of smiling young people – from a range of backgrounds, faiths and nationalities – absorbed in rich and vivid learning activities and replaced it with the image of an old wooden school desk from a bygone period. He changed the image of education and made learning look like drudgery. This book will help you to see a different picture and join an underground guerrilla movement; one that links the science of pedagogy with the art of pedagogy to discover the true heart of exceptional primary education. When I was involved in school inspections I loved to ask children, 'Why is your teacher special?' Too often this question was met with silence. Any child with a guerilla teacher would definitely have an answer!

I have had the privilege of seeing Jonathan lead training sessions for teachers. I have heard him speak with passion about how guerrilla teachers inspire young people. I have also witnessed the bizarre set of props he carries around with him in his battered suitcase. I started with a quotation that captures his classroom and so I thought I would finish with another that describes the kind of teacher he is. Jonathan Smith once wrote, 'As a teacher you're not only a writer, but an actor, a parent, a director and an improviser – it's not so much a Hollywood epic as a low-budget movie with a hand-held camera.' But the budget and camera don't really matter, it's what you do with them that counts; if you have the vision you can achieve great things.

Now that's Jonathan! I hope you enjoy the book. I did.

References:

Richard Arrowsmith, 'A Right Performance' in Denis Gleeson and Chris Husbands, *The Performing School*. London: Routledge, 2001.

Stephen Phillips, 'Frank McCourt', *TES*, 25 November 2005. Available at: https://www.tes.co.uk/article.aspx?storycode=2169815.

Jonathan Smith, *The Learning Game: A Teacher's Inspirational Story*. London: Little, Brown and Company, 2000.

ACKNOWLEDGEMENTS

I've been incredibly lucky to have encountered a huge number of people who have helped me throughout my career. First and foremost, my thanks go to my family, especially my mum, dad and brother, who, through their love and support, have given me everything I could ever have wanted or needed.

Big thanks to all the incredibly talented people at Independent Thinking for their inspiration, support and friendship. Thanks to Caroline, Bev and everyone else at the Independent Thinking Press for their help and encouragement with this book, and to Julie, Pippa and Jacqui in the Independent Thinking office for effortlessly organising me and generally keeping me on the right track. To Nina, for giving me confidence when I first set out, and especially to Ian, for believing that I had something worthwhile to say, and for giving me the opportunity to say it.

A huge thank you to the colleagues I've worked with over the years, none more so than Fiona, who has not only tolerated my failings, but has been one of my biggest supporters and a constant source of encouragement. To Andy, because nothing is ever too much trouble; Lynne, for being one of the most supportive and thoughtful people I know; and to Tricia, a sounding board and one of the best teachers I've ever seen. Thank you to all of the children I've been privileged to teach during my time at St Catherine's – I think you've probably taught me an awful lot more than I have taught you! To the teaching assistants who have put up with countless unusual and bizarre requests while continuing to do their very best for the children, and in particular to Gary, a great teaching assistant, but an even better bloke. Rest in peace, Mr M.

Finally, to Will, a colleague, friend and mentor. Thank you for your encouragement, wisdom and guidance, which has brought me to this point.

CONTENTS

INTRODUCTION

'Unless someone like you cares a whole awful lot, nothing is going to get better. It's not.'

Dr Seuss

I didn't mean to write a book. I always thought that writing was something that real teachers didn't have time for.

Real teachers, the ones who teach real children in actual schools, are always up to their eyeballs in a whole host of important things that they know they need to do, and probably a number of unimportant things that they feel they have to do.

I am very much in this boat.

I can't quite pinpoint the moment I knew something had to change. Up until recently, I'd happily left it to those on high to make the big decisions on education, while I got on with the business of teaching children. But then the interfering started. It took different forms – from ever-changing Ofsted frameworks, to the new primary curriculum, until all of a sudden, the things that I held dear about education were under threat.

Part of me wished that I'd become a head teacher, because head teachers are important, and they can change things. I know this because my wife is a head teacher, and she's very important. Maybe, if I were a head teacher, I could do something about it. Head teachers have a vision. They have to; it's compulsory. And if you've got a vision, then you've got a chance.

It didn't take long before I developed some vision-envy. I started to think that if I had a vision of my own, then I wouldn't have to wait around for things to change; I could get on with it myself.

Then I remembered that I did have a vision; I'd just forgotten it.

In fact, we all have one.

If teaching is something you chose, and you've stuck at it for a while, then it's more than likely that you're in it for the right reasons.

As a young teacher, I wanted to make a difference to the lives of children; I wanted them to leave school as great people ready to tackle any of the challenges that life threw at them. It sounds idealistic, but I suppose that's the point of a vision.

The problem is that it's easy to get worn down; it's easy to lose sight of the vision. A child is not 3 per cent: a child is a child, and at the moment, they really, really need us to stand up for them.

This book is about a revolution. Not a flag-waving, drum-beating revolution, but an underground revolution, a classroom revolution. It's not about changing policy or influencing government; it's about doing what we know to be right, regardless of what we're told. It's a book for people on the ground: people in real classrooms, working with real children, trying to make a real difference.

This book is about regaining our vision.

And as the saying goes, 'If you can't beat them, go underground and beat them anyway.'

PART I
Starting a Revolution

Chapter 1

REVOLUTIONARY MOVEMENTS

Starting a revolution could be seen as a big step, and it would definitely be a risky thing to do without first doing some serious groundwork. To save time, I've drawn together (from literally minutes of research) what seem to be the qualities that are common to all good guerrillas.

In terms of recruitment, education has traditionally always been about qualifications. While some people might argue that we should be employing the most academically gifted and highly qualified people to teach our young people, others might recall the chemistry teacher they had at secondary school who, despite having a PhD, intensely disliked children, and couldn't teach his way out of a paper bag.

I think it's about time we cut out all of the uncertainty tied up with qualifications and instead, went for a much more robust system of personality cross-matching to see whether or not potential recruits have what it takes.

For starters, it seems that effective guerrillas fall into one of four types.

Thinkers, schemers and leaders

You like to plan ahead, and pride yourself on being prepared for any eventuality. Your organisational skills make you the go-to person in a crisis, and you've got a natty spreadsheet that's got the whole staff's tea and coffee requirements mapped out for ease of reference.

Militants, rabble-rousers and rule-breakers

You don't suffer fools and you're passionate about what you do. You're a committed, all-action, no-nonsense teaching machine, and – though no one would say it to your face – there's probably some borderline anger management issues bubbling under the surface there too.

Oddballs, mavericks and crackpots

You live life on the edge and love nothing better than flying by the seat of your (novelty) pants. Anything could happen in your classroom – and it frequently does. You continue to believe in unicorns, no matter what the scientists say.

Charmers, chancers and dreamers

You're unflappable, resourceful and optimistic.

You can expertly wriggle out of even the tightest of situations with your charm, ingenuity and unfathomably great hair.

If you don't associate yourself with any of the guerrilla gorilla types (did you see what I did there?), then guerrilla teaching is clearly not for you. Put the book down, step away, and go back to doing what you've always done with your pile of pre-prepared worksheets, run-of-the-mill pants and lacklustre hair.

If, on the other hand, you felt the warm glow of familiarity on reading these descriptions, then you could be just the kind of individual to make a difference.

Rather than strongly identifying with any one group (which, to be honest, would be a bit of a cause for concern), it's more likely that you've got a little bit of everything in there – a potent combination of the best bits.

Perhaps you're an optimistic planner and doer who's open to moments of creative madness? Or maybe you're a no-nonsense organiser with great hair who likes a bit of dressing up?

Regardless of your individual profile, if you're in some way channelling the spirit of a guerrilla, then you're well on the way to becoming just the kind of revolutionary our children need.

Welcome to the gang.

There ain't no 'I' in team

As formidable as any individual guerrilla teacher would be, there's no doubt that the business of starting a revolution is a group activity. There is no 'I' in team, and while, disappointingly, there's also no 'we', we'll definitely be stronger together than apart. Imagine a network of guerrilla teachers working subversively towards a common goal – a shared vision. We'd be unstoppable.

Now, before we get too carried away, we need to tighten a few things up. The beauty of guerrilla tactics lies in the ability to work with whatever resources we've got, no matter how ramshackle, shoddy or sparse they may be.

We can wait for as long as we want for things to change for the better, but while we're doing that, we may as well get on with taking what we've got, however rubbish we might think it is, and turning it into something that's amazing.

The best definition that I've come across for the word guerrilla goes like this:

To be a member of an unofficial group of combatants using the element of surprise to harass a larger less mobile target.[1]

There aren't many things I can think of that are as large and immobile as our education system, and if there was ever something that was long overdue a spot of harassment, then this is it.

Like some strange kind of military duck, our job is to appear normal and calm on the surface, while underneath, we'll be furiously causing all manner of nuisance to make sure that our children get the education they deserve.

---

1 I can't find the dictionary that has this definition (it was online and quite a while ago). The closest I could get to a source is from here: http://www.ukessays.com/essays/history/origin-of-guerrilla-warfare-history-essay.php. All the elements of the phrase are there but it's not a direct quote.

Chapter 2

TURN LEFT FOR BOATS, TRAINS, ELEPHANTS, FISH AND CASTLES

There's no point going guerrilla and causing a whole lot of trouble if we're not entirely clear about where we're going.

Not so long ago, while desperately trying to find a hotel deep in the heart of the Lake District, I was distracted by the most impressive road sign I've ever come across.

I didn't know that this much excitement could possibly exist in one place.

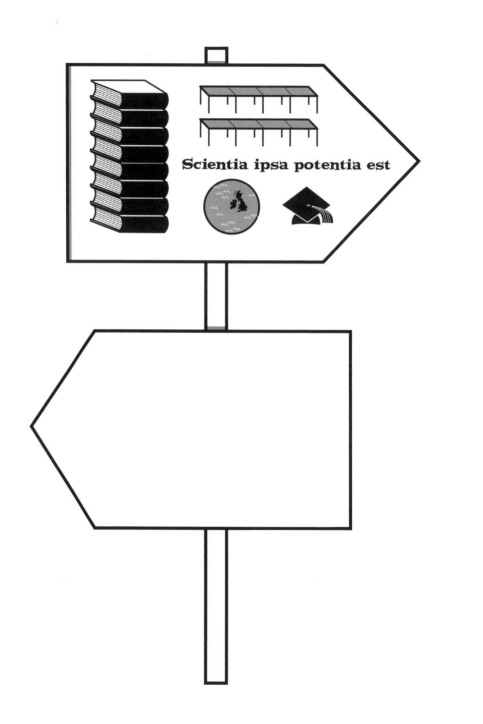

I'd defy anyone not to turn left – it looks unbelievable. After I posted the picture on Twitter, it got a response from fellow teacher Jim Smith (@lazyteacher), who suggested that it'd be a great way of thinking about schools. If this was the signpost that pointed to your school, what five symbols would you include? What if the signpost was pointing towards the education system?

In the current climate, it might look a bit like this.

But what kind of signpost would you want?

What do we want for the children we teach? What do we value? What is our vision of education in the twenty-first century?

If you've got a few minutes, have a doodle on the blank signpost and see what you come up with.

Without knowing exactly which symbols or ideas you've thought of, we can probably make some pretty safe bets. I would guess, or hope, that there are still some books on there. If not books, then some other symbol that represents knowledge. Even though I'm happy to accept the label of 'one of them creative types', I'm also a big fan of knowing stuff.

As for the other symbols, chances are they represent the broad and balanced education that we know our children need. Smiley faces (representing happiness, fun and laughter), thought bubbles or question marks (for curiosity), footsteps (for lifelong learning) or a handshake (for collaboration).

While there are countless symbols that you could have chosen (and no real wrong answers, unless you drew something rude), it's likely that we all value very similar things. We know what we want, and if we turned our signposts into a written statement, it could very well look like this:

Our vision is an education system that prepares our children for life in the twenty-first century by creating opportunities for learning that are engaging, motivating and memorable.

Our vision is a system that encourages independence, curiosity and creativity: a system that produces collaborators, innovators, leaders and, above all, a system that helps our children to understand what it means to be human.

Simple. Now all we've got to do is get there.

Chapter 3

GUERRILLA THINKING

So we've got a vision, shared aims, and now we're forming the beginnings of a new revolutionary movement.

You may have realised by now that this isn't actually a book – it's more of a recruitment drive. So, in total confidence that you're coming along with me, let's get on with the *how*.

One of the biggest problems teachers face is the curriculum itself, and to understand the size of the challenge, we need a bit of historical background (this bit's short – stick with me).

At the end of the nineteenth century, education became compulsory for all. This developed into an education system that prepared children for roles in the new industrialised age.

In 1944, state-funded education was arranged into a structure containing three types of school: grammar schools, secondary technical schools and secondary modern schools. Children were then packed off to their respective schools according to academic performance via the famous eleven plus exam (a bit like the sorting hat in Harry Potter films). The system was designed to meet the economic needs of the country and to provide a workforce. It was also meant to break down class barriers, with education available to everyone regardless of background. This all sounds brilliant, and, for its time, maybe it was. The problem now is that not a lot has changed.

The three-part system has gone, but there's still a big emphasis on academia and the idea that people can be classified as either academic or non-academic. There've been a few attempts to change this thinking along the way, and in 1999, the National Advisory Committee on Creative and Cultural Education (NACCCE), headed by Sir Ken Robinson, was given the job of addressing the challenge of developing the creative talents of all. In its report, called 'All Our Futures: Creativity, Culture and Education',[1] Sir Ken talked about a national strategy for creative and cultural education. Its aim was to 'develop young people's capacities

---

1 NACCCE, All Our Futures: Creativity, Culture and Education (1999).

for original ideas and action ... to enable them to engage positively with the growing complexity and diversity of social values and ways of life.' Which, when you read it, doesn't sound a million miles away from our vision.

The report highlighted the need for new priorities in education rather than holding on to the industrial ideals of the past. At the time, it went down a storm, particularly within the business and education worlds, but despite its wise words, it hasn't led to the reforms – let alone transformation – that are needed.

In 2009 there was a brief glimpse of light at the end of the tunnel with the publication of the Independent Review of the Primary Curriculum by Sir Jim Rose.[2] The report seemed to highlight exactly the kind of things that would achieve our vision. A combination of knowledge and skills. Direct subject teaching, alongside the opportunity to apply and use these skills across the curriculum. A broad, balanced and blended curriculum. But, just as we started to feel a little optimistic about a shift in thinking, all was lost – thanks to an untimely change in government.

'Nothing is more dangerous than an idea, when you only have one idea': I don't think French philosopher and journalist Émile Chartier was referring directly to the current state of education when he said this, but he might as well have been.

Within what felt like a very short space of time, we were faced with what appeared to be a huge step backwards in the content and purpose of the national curriculum. Unashamedly borrowing from the work of E.D. Hirsch and his writing on cultural literacy, the new framework aimed to 'provide pupils with an introduction to the core knowledge that they need to be educated citizens.'[3]

This core knowledge is pretty extensive, and while you can't deny its importance, there's more to education than just knowing facts.

In geography, for example, the idea that filling children's heads with information about different countries will ensure they appreciate the richness of other cultures is hugely simplistic. I've got nothing against geography, but to appreciate

---

2 Jim Rose. *Independent Review of the Primary Curriculum Final Report.* (DCSF Publications: 2009). Available at: http://www.educationengland.org.uk/documents/pdfs/2009-IRPC-final-report.pdf.

3 Department for Education. *The National Curriculum in England Key Stages 1 and 2 Framework Document 2013.* Available at: https://www.gov.uk/government/uploads/system/uploads/attachment_data/file/425601/PRIMARY_national_curriculum.pdf.

other cultures requires the ability to explore issues from different perspectives, to show empathy, and to recognise our role and responsibilities as global citizens, none of which are solely geographical skills.

If we're going to challenge this knowledge-driven compartmentalisation of learning (not sure that's a real word but it definitely should be!), then we'll have to do it by subversively adding back the skills that have been stripped out of our current curriculum; the kinds of skills that, along with knowledge, will best prepare our children for the future.

This should be easy. Or it would be if it weren't for the fact that the future has a habit of being a bit unpredictable. We have no real idea what the future will hold. There are very few certainties: we know that our children will have to be able to communicate effectively with others, but we have no idea just *how* they will communicate. We also know that they will face an increasingly competitive employment market, and it's a decent bet that they will change jobs numerous times. What those jobs might be is, again, anyone's guess.

Trying to make predictions about the future is a pretty risky business, even for those who are good at it. In 1945, Sir Arthur C. Clarke, the British science fiction writer, inventor and futurist, correctly predicted that, one day, satellites would be used in orbit to form a global communications network. This seemed an incredible statement at the time, particularly given the fact that Alexander Graham Bell had only invented the telephone sixty-nine years earlier. Having said that, Sir Arthur also had his off days. In 1966, he predicted that by the year 2000, 'houses will be able to fly … The time may come, therefore, when whole communities may migrate south in the winter'.[4]

Given the hit and miss nature of this predicting business, we should probably leave it well alone and focus instead on ensuring that our children develop the skills needed to adapt to whatever the future throws at them. In the supposed words of Eric Hoffer:

In a time of drastic change it is the learners who inherit the future. The learned usually find themselves equipped to live in a world that no longer exists.

---

4 Arthur C. Clarke, *The View from Serendip* (London: Macmillan, 1979).

Fortunately, we're not breaking new ground here, and there are plenty of things that can help with this process.

One of the most useful resources I've come across is the Personal Learning and Thinking Skills framework, or PLTS. The PLTS was originally intended as a document for Key Stages (KS) 3 and 4 and, as it says in the dim and dark national archive, 'was developed (by the Qualifications and Curriculum Authority; QCA) and refined over a number of years in consultation with employers, parents, schools, students and the wider public.'[5] For those relatively new to teaching, this was from a time when government consultation involved some degree of listening, as opposed to the more recent working model of 'ask and ignore'.

The framework aimed to capture the skills that, along with English, maths and information and communications technology (ICT), are essential to success in learning, life and work.

The skills were divided up as follows.

Independent enquirers

Young people process and evaluate information in their investigations, planning what to do and how to go about it. They take informed and well-reasoned decisions, recognising that others have different beliefs and attitudes.

Can:
- identify questions to answer and problems to resolve
- plan and carry out research, appreciating the consequences of decisions
- explore issues, events and problems from different perspectives
- analyse and evaluate information, judging its relevance and value
- consider the influence of circumstances, beliefs and feelings on decisions and events
- support conclusions using reasoned arguments and evidence.

---

5   QCA. *A framework of personal, learning and thinking skills.* Available at: http://webarchive. nationalarchives.gov.uk/20110223175304/http:/curriculum.qcda.gov.uk/key-stages-3-and-4/ skills/personal-learning-and-thinking-skills/index.aspx.

Creative thinkers

Young people think creatively by generating and exploring ideas, making original connections. They try different ways to tackle a problem, working with others to find imaginative solutions and outcomes that are of value.

Can:

- generate ideas and explore possibilities
- ask questions to extend their thinking
- connect their own and others' ideas and experiences in inventive ways
- question their own and others' assumptions
- try out alternatives or new solutions and follow ideas through
- adapt ideas as circumstances change.

Reflective learners

Young people evaluate their strengths and limitations, setting themselves realistic goals with criteria for success. They monitor their own performance and progress, inviting feedback from others and making changes to further their learning.

Can:

- assess themselves and others, identifying opportunities and achievements
- set goals with success criteria for their development and work
- review progress, acting on the outcomes
- invite feedback and deal positively with praise, setbacks and criticism
- evaluate experiences and learning to inform future progress
- communicate their learning in relevant ways for different audiences.

Team workers

Young people work confidently with others, adapting to different contexts and taking responsibility for their own part. They listen to and take account of different views. They form collaborative relationships, resolving issues to reach agreed outcomes.

Can:

- collaborate with others to work towards common goals
- reach agreement and manage discussions to achieve results
- adapt behaviour to suit different roles and situations, including leadership roles
- show fairness and consideration to others
- take responsibility, showing confidence in themselves and their contribution
- provide constructive support and feedback to others.

Self-managers

Young people organise themselves, showing personal responsibility, initiative, creativity and enterprise with a commitment to learning and self-improvement. They actively embrace change, responding positively to new priorities, coping with challenges and looking for opportunities.

Can:

- seek out challenges or new responsibilities and show flexibility when priorities change
- work towards a goal showing initiative, commitment and perseverance
- organise time and resources, prioritising actions
- anticipate, take and manage risks
- deal with competing pressures, including personal and work-related demands
- respond positively to change, seeking advice and support when needed
- manage their emotions, and build and maintain relationships.

Effective participators

Young people actively engage in issues that affect them and those around them. They play a full part in the life of the school, college, workplace or wider community by taking responsible action to bring improvements for others as well as themselves.

(I think, although it's not explicitly mentioned, there should also be something in here about young people viewing themselves as global citizens.)

Can:

- discuss issues of concern, seeking resolution where needed
- present a persuasive cause for action
- propose practical ways forward, breaking these down into manageable steps
- identify improvements that would benefit others as well as themselves
- try to influence others, negotiating and balancing diverse views to reach workable solutions
- act as an advocate for views and beliefs that may differ from their own.

In child-friendly speak, the skills would look as shown on the Guerrilla Guide to Learning and Thinking Skills wheel.

When you look around the wheel, there are a few things that stand out. Some of these skills are taught explicitly in schools: 'Listen and speak', for example (managing discussions), might be explored through work on debate in English, or 'Explain your thinking' (supporting conclusions with evidence) through investigative work in science or maths.

However, others form part of the hidden curriculum – the stuff that's not explicitly taught, and probably never appears on a planning sheet. We all want children to develop these skills, but the problem with them being hidden is that quite often they go missing or, worse still, disappear altogether.

One of the key areas that seems to have fallen victim to this is, arguably, creative thinking. Now, I say 'arguably' because I have no real evidence for this, other than the fact I've been teaching young people now for nearly eighteen years and it seems to be the single biggest area that they struggle with. We've got pretty good in primary schools at developing collaborative learners, and we quite

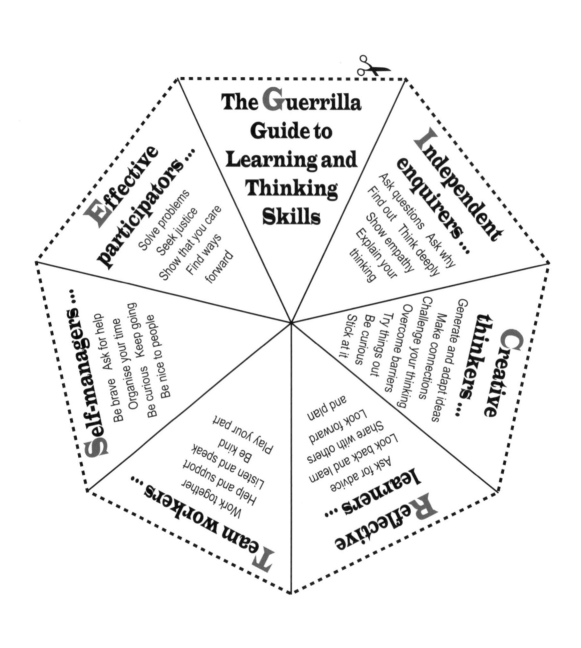

The **G**uerrilla Guide to Learning and Thinking Skills

Effective participators ...
Solve problems
Seek justice
Show that you care
Find ways forward

Independent enquirers ...
Ask questions Ask why
Find out Think deeply
Show empathy
Explain your thinking

Self-managers ...
Be brave Ask for help
Organise your time
Be curious Keep going
Be nice to people

Creative thinkers ...
Generate and adapt ideas
Make connections
Challenge your thinking
Overcome barriers
Try things out
Be curious
Stick at it

Team workers ...
Work together
Help and support
Listen and speak
Be kind
Play your part

Reflective learners ...
Ask for advice
Look back and learn
Share with others
Look forward and plan

naturally build in opportunities for children to explain their thinking and reflect. There are other areas, too, where I can identify with children and classes who excelled. I can remember the young girl who decided that we should all complete a Sport Relief mile, persuaded her classmates, ordered the resources, and raised a heap of money – all because she cared. Or the class which worked as a team to rehearse and perform their own end-of-year show. But when it comes to creative thinkers, it's more of a struggle. If we're honest, how many of our Year 6 leavers would we describe as being insatiably curious? How many are experts at making connections and overcoming barriers?

It's not that the children I teach never turn out to be creative thinkers – it's just that those who do seem to be few and far between and, to be honest, it seems to be in spite of what we do in school rather than because of it.

One of the rare examples I can remember involves a young man who can only be described as my nemesis. I'm going to withhold his name (mainly in case he ever tracks me down in the future). He was eleven years old when I taught him, small for his age, and had a permanent mischievous twinkle in his eye. Throughout school, he has left behind a trail of shell-shocked teachers who were unable to cope with his own special brand of non-conformity. In Year 5, he managed to fiddle a reward system based on collecting counters. Sitting as he was in his own special seat, right under the teacher's nose, he pretended to accidentally knock off a counter pot belonging to a rival group. Apologising to the teacher, he set about picking them up from the floor. When the counters were back in the pot, he calmly returned to his seat. With the teacher lulled into a false sense of security, he started to remove stolen counters he'd collected from the sole of his shoes thanks to the carefully placed coloured adhesive tack he'd secretly added earlier. With his additional counters, the weekly prize was his for the taking.

There are countless other examples of further misadventures, my favourite of which I can't write about for legal reasons, but resulted in him having his military-spec night-vision goggles confiscated by the head teacher.

He's one of those kids who drives teachers to absolute distraction, but if I had to choose someone to solve a problem that my life depended on, he would be top of my list by a mile. This young man is an incredibly creative thinker. Watching him make connections, try alternatives and overcome barriers is inspiring. He has the potential to be hugely successful – yet we tried throughout his school life to subdue his skills. The fact that his creativity has been channelled into trouble-making is more a reflection on the system than it is on him. Now don't get me wrong – I don't mean to absolve him of any responsibility; there were plenty of times when he was, quite rightly, in plenty of trouble, but when he was able to use his skills productively, he was a perfect pupil.

This young man is exceptional. He's not the only child I've come across to demonstrate high levels of creative thinking, but he's definitely in the minority. He's managed to maintain his ability to think creatively despite us. Now we've just got to worry about the other 90-odd per cent who haven't.

Chapter 4

GUERRILLA HQ

'There is no doubt that creativity is the most important human resource of all. Without creativity, there would be no progress, and we would be forever repeating the same patterns.'

Edward de Bono[1]

Being able to think creatively is clearly a big deal. If you look at the other sections on the skills wheel (page 20), or even back at your signpost, I think developing creative thinking is a key driver for developing the vast majority of the other areas we're interested in. If we can crack this, then we're well on the way to producing the unstoppable young people we're after.

Now, before we get carried away, we're still surrounded by rubbish. And working with what we've got means we have to be looking at *how* we teach rather than *what* we teach.

It seems to make sense that if we value creative thinking, and want to actively promote it in our children, then we need to be creative teachers ourselves. A lot of what we do in schools relies on modelling. We've got something we want the children to learn, so we model it for them. It follows, then, that if we want our children to develop their creative thinking, we should, at least to begin with, look no further than ourselves.

Having undertaken the personality cross-matching test from earlier on, you're probably in possession of an awful lot of the attributes that you'll need to give our children the education they deserve. To get to grips with exactly what this takes, we're going to have to go a bit deeper and take a look at the guerrilla teacher's brain.

You may well have come across various different bits of information about the brain during your time as a teacher, although probably not during your teacher training (which, by and large, seems to ignore this fairly important organ). To

---

1   Edward de Bono, *Sur/petition: Going Beyond Competition* (London: HarperCollins, 1993), p. 169.

get us up to speed, and to help cut through the mountains of research into neuroscience, I'll use my own highly academic model to help explain the inner workings of the guerrilla teacher.

The guerrilla brain is the nerve centre of our whole operation, and as a result, from here on in, I'll refer to it as guerrilla *head*quarters (I was over the moon when I thought of this), or GHQ for short.

As everyone knows, the brain can be split neatly into three sections that represent the three floors of GHQ:

Floor 1: The ground floor – this is the bit in charge of all the stuff we do without thinking. (Chapters 5–7)

Floor 2: The first floor – this is the bit where we think about stuff. (Chapters 8–9)

Floor 3: The rooftop terrace – the bit where we think about risky, scary, 'sky's the limit' type stuff. (Chapters 10–12)

For the guerrilla teacher, each of these sections has a particular part to play in going about the business of educating our young people.

As you can see from the diagram, the different sections of GHQ deal with different elements of being a guerrilla teacher. The ground floor is involved with those hard to pin down but massively important traits that all great guerrilla teachers have. I suppose they could be described as attributes or values – or even summed up as 'personality'. Above that, we move up to the first floor where we think about creative teaching (modelling creative thinking for the children) before finally reaching the rooftop terrace, where we think about the tough stuff, creative learning (letting the children have a go for themselves).

To keep things simple, I'm going to tackle the make-up of a guerrilla teacher from the bottom up.

The Guerrilla Brain (GHQ)

PART II
Guerrilla HQ

Chapter 5

THE GROUND FLOOR: TEACHER PERSONA

The idea of teachers having a personality could be considered pretty progressive in some circles, and there are teachers out there who don't seem to believe that it's that important. Fortunately, even for those who are a bit lacking (don't point, it's rude), it's rare that the persona you see at the front of the class is an exact representation of the personality that lies beneath.

Part of being a teacher is putting yourself out there – up at the front, under the watchful gaze of the eager young people in front of you. Because of this, teachers exaggerate aspects of personality, or sometimes even fake them if they're not there. This has something to do with the performer hidden somewhere in all of us. I'm generally a quiet person. I don't particularly like being in big groups of people and I'd rather be at home watching *The Great British Bake Off* than at a wild party. In front of a group of children, though, a switch is flicked and I portray the teacher that I want children to see. When I first realised this was happening, it made me worry that I was just putting on an act or deceiving the children in some way. Now, I think that it's not just OK, but essential. For example, what if I was a really miserable person; a total pessimist? Now, it's unlikely that you would choose life as a teacher if you are one of these 'glass half-empty' people, but some do slip through the net. In life, there's something about this attitude that I find quite appealing, and in the A.A. Milne *Winnie the Pooh* stories, my favourite character was always Eeyore. While there may well be teachers out there who share his world view, if push came to shove, would I want my own children to be taught by a pessimistic teacher? Absolutely not. I'd want the teacher to pretend to be happy and get on with spreading joy as opposed to gloom.

Obviously, this switching between normal persona and teacher persona works in reverse too. While we might enthusiastically praise our children for sitting smartly and showing us 'magnet' eyes, it doesn't work as well with your partner at home.

Teacher persona is about the image we want to project in the classroom.

How do I want the children to see me? What kind of teacher do I want to be?

When working with students, or newly qualified teachers (NQTs), the biggest single worry for lots of them is, *How do I look like a teacher? How do I get that presence in the classroom?*

To start with, the answer might be, 'Pretend'. Pretend you're confident; practise walking with your head held high and your shoulders back, practise issuing instructions to family and friends in an assertive, yet positive, voice. From the moment we walk into the room, we need to appear confident, decisive and in control. Regardless of personality, if we lack confidence, we lack presence, and if we lack presence, we're in trouble.

Just to complicate matters, it's also possible to mess things up with the opposite approach. Regardless of your stance on the whole traditional/progressive thing, if you stroll into a classroom on day one, and announce, 'Hey guys, we're about to set off on a learning journey – hold on to your hats! Oh, and call me Johnny,' the chances are, you won't make it through the term.

First things first. We get our presence right, and get the children responding. It's a long-term strategy: if we set out our stall early, it'll open up incredible opportunities later in the year.

I love the first couple of weeks of term. I love walking into my empty classroom on the first morning, with all the neatly arranged pencils in pots on tables and books out in places so the children know straight away where to sit. Just before I open the door, the music will go on. Three tracks (the same ones every morning) that make me smile, or – on a really good day – dance. I talk a lot in the first few weeks. I think teachers have to. I don't want to get into the rights and wrongs of teacher talk right now, but in the first few weeks, it's our opportunity to set the tone for the year.

Building foundations is really important. In time, I want the children to be able to work creatively, collaboratively and independently. I want them to take responsibility for their learning, for us to work and learn together. But for all of these complex things to happen, the culture and climate of the classroom must be right.

When we think about modelling in school, we tend to think in terms of explaining a concept within a lesson, but in reality, it's much, much more important than that. Everything we do – our language, phraseology, demeanour, outlook, body language, responses and reactions – every little ounce of the teacher we present is being modelled for our children. Lots of this we don't even think about: it's the ground floor of GHQ running the show like it's on autopilot. Given the impact that our teacher persona has on our children, however, it's definitely something we shouldn't leave to chance, and so before we get to the teaching bit, there are certain universal attributes and qualities we should consciously display from the moment the children walk in the room.

Interest and importance

I want the children to know that I'm interested in things. Really interested. I want them to know that I'm interested in them, and that they are the single most important thing in the room. I want to show them that I'm interested in the world, the stuff outside the classroom windows, things that are on the news. Some of this can be done deliberately through the magic of show and tell.

I first came across this phenomenon while teaching a reception class. It basically does exactly what it says on the tin: children bring things in, and then talk about them. Sometimes it might just be a bit of news. It's something I've done with all classes throughout my career. Even in Year 6, with all the pressures of fitting things in, the one part of the timetable that is ever present is show and tell. Some people might argue that it wastes valuable teaching time, but the power of knowing your children and building in dedicated time to model listening, interest, curiosity, fascination and joy should never be underestimated. Sometimes it can be outrageously funny (which is no bad way to start the day), and at other times heart-warmingly poignant and affirming.

To make sure that you're not left out, it's always a good thing to be ready with a couple of stories of your own. These should be genuine, true stories about your life (maybe with a bit of embellishment), but should definitely not include any of the weird stuff you might get up to behind closed doors. To spice things up a bit further, I always check up on the news (for particularly funny or strange stories) before school so I'm ready to throw one into the mix if we hit a lull. In terms of modelling, the language we use is really important: for example, 'You'll never guess what I saw on the news this morning – this is amazing'.

It's incredible how quickly this attitude rubs off on young people, and most mornings there'll be a group of them desperate to tell or show me something they have noticed for themselves.

Top five show-and-tell items

1. A kangaroo testicle key ring (same child as the night-vision goggles).

2. A shark's jawbone.

3. A 100-year-old letter that had been found behind a fireplace.

4. A Lego Elvis.

5. A giant African land snail.

For a couple of variations on the show-and-tell theme, you could also try these ideas.

Mystery object

Start a collection of bizarre and unusual objects. When you've got a decent range (see the list below for some ideas), pick one, and get the children to pretend that it's their show and tell. They have to make up what it is, what it's used for, where it came from and why they've got it. When several of them have had a go, the class could vote on their favourite/funniest/strangest version, and the winner gets to take it home as a prize! (When the game's been up and running for a while, encourage the children to bring in their own found objects to add to the pot.)

Here are five items to get you started:

1. A ballcock and float valve (ask your dad).

2. Handlebars off an old bike.

3. A hairdryer diffuser thing (the spiky dish-looking bit that goes on the end).

4. A cat flap.

5. A welly boot (just the one).

As well as being a useful way of keeping show and tell fresh, it also allows you to get rid of any rubbish you've got in your garage or loft without the need for an expensive skip. Win–win.

Tall tales

This is a bit of a dubious one, as it encourages a bit of fib-telling on the part of the children, but if you can get over the fact that you're encouraging lying, then you're on to a winner.

Have one day each week dedicated to making up something. Popular choices include getting the children to come up with excuses for things they haven't done:

I haven't done my homework because …

I was late for school because …

I haven't got my equipment because …

I can't go to detention because …

If you're still worried about the ethics of this, you could always stick the activity in your planning file and call it transition work!

Using show and tell lets our children know that we're interested in them. It automatically makes them feel important, and to make the most of this there are a couple of other techniques that will really help to hammer it home.

Lesson by lesson

Mid-lesson, there might be an interesting response from a child so you revert to the same kind of positive script you modelled when telling them about the news story: 'That's really interesting, what a brilliant thing to know – we should find out more about that … Let's add it to the "Stuff to think about" wall.' Without much effort, and before very long, you not only build a brilliant relationship with the class, but are in a position to make connections between the different points of interest. In lessons, you'll naturally feed in personalised elements that relate directly to the children and, as a result, they'll hang on your every word.

Ignoring people

This is where we adopt a bit of guerrilla-style intolerance. What happens if the head teacher or a member of the leadership team – or, in fact, anyone – appears at your classroom door with a message? In the vast majority of cases, we stop what we're doing (teaching) and allow the person to speak. Subconsciously, we're telling the children that although we bang on about learning being important, it's not anywhere near as important as hearing that this afternoon's assembly has been moved to 2.30pm.

Instead, think of it as a standoff. Make them wait. Finish what you're doing, teach the bit you're teaching, wait for a natural break, then go and see what they want. If it's not that important (which is the case on 95 per cent of occasions) then they'll probably just go. If it is important, then they might write you a note, or even interrupt (no bad thing, as it's *their* interruption rather than your stopping that's got in the way of things). It might seem a sure-fire way to annoy people, but it gives a powerful message to the young people in the room about our priorities – without having to say a word. If you're worried about upsetting people (particularly the boss), catch up with them afterwards, apologise for ignoring them and explain your strategy. Before long, you'll have the majority of message-bringers trained up and fully expecting to be ignored.

Taking the moral high ground

If you're acting on the advice above, then you're well on the way to creating the perfect climate in your classroom. If we can communicate with every fibre of our being just how much we care about them and their learning, then we're in the perfect position to take the higher ground on those occasions where things go wrong.

Again, this means reverting to scripts. For individuals:

'You're [name behaviour: shouting out/wandering around/distracting your partner, etc.]. It's getting in the way of our learning. You need to stop. Thank you.'

(It should always be 'thank you' at the end, and not 'please' – one of the simplest and best tips I was ever given as a new teacher.)

For the class:

'We need to stop for a minute. I want you to remember that the most important thing in this room is you and your learning – I won't let anything get in the way of that.'

Regardless of the actual words we use (try making up your own scripts), we can always bring it back to learning, and the fact that we care so much about it that we're not prepared to be thrown off course by unimportant or uninteresting stuff.

Happiness and optimism

I want the children to know that I'm a happy person, and I want them to know that happiness is contagious. I've already talked about the fact that nobody wants to go to work and be faced by miserableness every morning, and children are no different. Thanks to my morning songs, even if I'm tired and fed up, there's always a smile on my face as the children come in (it's definitely something to try unless you're into hard-core techno – or Leonard Cohen). There isn't anything that beats a smile to convey the message that we're happy to be there, and if you can't muster one as the children come in, you're in the wrong job.

When we've mastered the morning smile, the children won't be able to resist smiling back (it's virtually impossible) and we're already set up for the day.

Along with the smile (which should be our default setting), language also plays a part. I don't just want children sitting ready to learn, I want children sitting, *smiling* and ready to learn, and so this feeds straight into my classroom management scripts:

'Let me see those beautiful smiling faces – that's stunning – are we ready to start?'

For the tough and the streetwise, we can throw in a bit of personalisation and humour:

'I'm looking at you, Kyle! Where's that smile? Show me those teeth!'

And Kyle will do it because we have a good relationship, and we have a good relationship because he knows I'm interested in him, and he knows I'm interested in him because I asked him about his new dog when he came into the classroom first thing this morning, and I mentioned his dog because I'd remembered he'd spoken about it last week in show and tell when we were busy wasting valuable learning time. Perfect.

Curiosity, awe and wonder

Curious people get distracted. You might have just nipped outside to put the wheelie bin out, but you notice the clear night sky, and before long you're happily lying on the roof of your car staring up at the stars. Interesting things happen all around – even at school. A colleague and good friend of mine, Will Ryan, tells a story about a helicopter that had to make a forced landing on a school field. You can imagine the state the children were in, but in most of the classes, blinds were quickly drawn so they could get back to their learning.

Having previously looked at how to create a climate where learning is the most important thing, it would seem that closing the blinds and focusing on the lesson in hand is the only course of action. If we apply a bit of common sense, though, the difference between an interruption from the head teacher and a helicopter landing should be perfectly clear. Head teachers and their messages are to be ignored – helicopters are not. I suppose that it's to do with potential. I've never had a message delivered to my classroom that had endless scope for learning. A helicopter, on the other hand, not only grabs your attention, but offers massive opportunity for a whole host of interesting stuff.

If we miss or ignore opportunities to model curiosity and wonder, then we'll gradually knock that sense of awe and curiosity out of our children. We have to deviate from the plan; we have to embrace tangents and seek out opportunities. Sadly there aren't many helicopters, but there are other things that grab our children's attention. Trying to teach against the backdrop of snowfall is nearly impossible. I don't care how good a teacher you are, the bottom line is that we're not nearly as interesting as snow, hail, thunder, torrential rain – or, on a bad day, light drizzle.

There's no point competing, so we may as well join in and turn the distraction into a learning opportunity. Better still, we should aim to be the very first face pressed up against the window, with the children scrabbling to keep up.

'Look at the size of those snowflakes – they're amazing. I wonder how many you could catch in your mouth? Do you want to try?'

Apparently, the most basic snow crystal geometry is a hexagonal prism, and these form incredible structures called stellar plates when the temperature drops to about −2 degrees. We should probably get back to learning something important, though.

When it starts to rain, the artist Andy Goldsworthy has the habit of lying very still on the floor. When it stops, he gets up, and left behind is the dry silhouette of his body. What about that for an outdoors version of sleeping lions?[1]

The deviation doesn't have to be about stopping everything and dashing outside. Sometimes it might just be a brief pause, or mid-lesson moment of wonderment (more on wonderings in Chapter 13):

'I wonder why that happened.'

'I wonder what would happen if …'

'What do you think of that? Isn't that amazing?'

Do we let the children know often enough that maths is beautiful, or that history is fascinating?

Stories are another powerful way of letting the children see that we're fascinated by seemingly ordinary things. I was never hugely bothered about mirrors or reflection in science, until I found out that, in 212 BC, legend has it that Archimedes used a series of tessellating hexagonal mirrors to focus the sun's rays, creating the world's first weaponised laser and incinerating the attacking Roman fleet. Imagine building that!

Whenever I'm teaching something new, I'll always do a bit of research to see if there's a similar little gem that I can throw in mid-lesson. I might not put it on the plan, and I might not always use it, but it's a powerful little device and it screams out to children that we're not interested in learning because there's stuff in the curriculum that they have to know, we're interesting in learning because there are incredible things out there just waiting to be discovered.

---

1 Also known as 'dead fishes', this is the game of choice for the under-pressure teacher: a good ten minutes of children lying on the floor, completely still and in total silence. Genius.

Modelling wonder is a key guerrilla trait – making the most of amazing things when they happen. Along with this, though, it's also our job to provide a bit of awe and wonder too. How many moments do you have in a year when something you do makes the class stop dead in their tracks? The kind of moments when jaws drop, or the only words the children can utter are, 'I can't believe that just happened'? If they're a bit thin on the ground, then try some of these classroom bombshells.

Top five jaw-dropping moments

1. Levitate (it's easier than you think – try looking it up on YouTube).

2. Smash an egg on a child's head (make sure it's a hollowed-out egg, and make sure you let the child in on the secret before you do it. I used this in a lesson on instructions – we were creating recipes and I was showing the children the different ingredients at the front when I pretended to trip, holding the egg, and smashed it on the nearest child's head. It's probably the best reaction I've ever had from a group of children – they were gobsmacked and then told everyone they saw, which unfortunately meant I couldn't repeat the trick the following year, as the secret was out!).

3. Produce handfuls of green slime from your nose (again, reliant on a bit of misdirection. Pretend to get a bit sniffly, and start building up for a sneeze, then turn your back, and secretly take out a handful of green slime from a pot concealed in your pocket. Go for a huge sneeze, then turn back to the children with your hands covering your nose and the green slime oozing between your fingers. Apologise profusely and offer to shake hands with as many children as you can. Admittedly, it might be more disgust rather than wonder, but it gets a brilliant reaction, and if you were interested in learning, it could be used to start some work on bacteria, micro-organisms or healthy living).

4. Build something really big – bigger than the children – something so big they can get inside it. Try a rocket, a pyramid, a Saxon village …

5. Blow something up. (If you're short on time, or a bit health-and-safety conscious, you could go down the 'Alka-Seltzer in a little plastic film canister' route. If you're after something a bit bigger, try taking out the

school greenhouse with a compressed air rocket launcher (instructions also on YouTube!). You'll achieve instant legend status with the children, and can always pass it off as an experiment gone wrong when the head teacher hauls you into their office.)

Playfulness

'Nonsense wakes up the brain cells.'

Dr Seuss

Included in this could also be daftness, humour, a sense of fun and imagination.

This is not necessarily day one stuff, but equally it's not that old line from teacher training about not smiling until Christmas. A teacher can't spend their year being the class clown, but it's massively important that children see school, and learning, as fun. I don't think it's day one stuff, because you have to test the waters. You have to know how the class is going to react. You have to start small. It's no good producing some full-on comedy performance if the children will either (a) react hysterically and fly out of control, or (b) cry because your 'wackiness' is frightening them.

Fortunately, the young people we teach don't have an overly sophisticated sense of humour, which means there are plenty of easy tricks that will get them laughing and engaged.

Joke of the day/week

Make them bad – Christmas cracker bad. Go for a groan if you can get it, while pretending that you find it hilarious. Do it often enough and the children will soon be joining in with their own. A note of caution, though – not all of our children have developed a clear understanding of appropriateness, as the following offering from a six-year-old at my wife's school demonstrates:

Child: Miss, how do you make a door laugh?

Teacher: I don't know. How do you make a door laugh?

Child: You tickle its knob!

Teacher: Oh, er, I think you mean handle, don't you?!

Double disaster! Not only can you guarantee that this will be the only thing about the school day that the rest of the class will remember when they go home, but our little budding comedy genius will now grow up thinking that the punchline to the joke should be 'handle'. Be careful. You have been warned!

Drop something

Drop something unbreakable, and then blame someone else for it. This is best done with a pause. Drop it, then stare at the dropped item in shock for a few seconds, then blame someone else, 'That was your fault, Kyle, you made me do that with your telepathic brain thingy' (if you're in any way unsure about how a child will react to being blamed, pick on your teaching assistant instead!).

Make them salute whenever they see you

I think this is probably standard practice in some posh private schools, and if it's good enough for them, then it's good enough for the rest of us. There are few things better than having your rank of guerrilla teacher recognised with a bit of military-style respect, and to achieve this, all you need to do is challenge your children to salute you the instant they see you around the school building. The effect this has is incredible – admittedly, it's more incredible for unsuspecting colleagues who might happen to witness it. It also has a lasting effect on visitors to the school, who really haven't got a clue what's going on. (For maximum effect, never explain it to anyone: just give a knowing nod, then march off in double time.)

In any given class, you'll have a hard core of children who will ensure that this routine is maintained throughout the whole year, so be prepared to keep it up. Oh, and don't forget to salute back – respect is a two-way thing.

Tell a story

Picking up on the show and tell idea from earlier, quick stories can be a great way of making children laugh. Build up a bank of good ones and bear in mind your target audience. (For five-year-olds, anything related to falling over is great; for older ones, make it a bit naughty.) Personal favourites over the years have included 'The haunted baby monitor', 'The close call with the cat and the sausage' and 'What the orang-utan did with the bottle'.

Do a magic trick (badly)

Tell them you're going to make something disappear.

1. Show them the object.
2. Get children to close their eyes.
3. Say the magic words.
4. Stuff object up jumper.
5. Have them open their eyes.
6. Hey presto – it's vanished.

Develop a big head

Another easy route into humour is to develop a bit of a big head. Now, this might not sound that desirable, but it's only done so that we can later set ourselves up for a fall. This borrows from the 'Oh no, he isn't' kind of pantomime routine that never fails to get a reaction from the audience. To start off with, we can use some throwaway remarks to test the waters and see how the children respond. Refer to yourself as the most handsome, most stunningly beautiful, brainiest or most talented teacher/person in the world. If they agree, then well done: you must be stunning and some kind of genius. What we're hoping for, though, is a bit of a giggle that tells us that they might disagree, leading to mock disbelief from us and the beginning of an ongoing joke.

To take this playfulness a bit further, I frequently tell the children that I'm a world-renowned expert in any number of different fields. While these are pretty wide-ranging (actor, inventor, break-dancer, rapper, opera singer, etc.), my current favourite area of self-professed expertise is in the art of Japanese paper folding.

Origami

Rather than just go for standard, run-of-the-mill origami, I tell the children that I'm the world record holder for Speed Origami. This involves the ability to produce any origami object in under five seconds. Again, you will get murmurings of disbelief, so I tell them that I can prove it. Turning my back to the class, they count down from five while I secretly screw up a piece of white paper into a ball. When the time's up, I proudly turn around to show off my creation – an origami cloud.

This can (and should) be repeated numerous times, obviously with a new creation each time. Alternatives are an origami snowball (again, white paper), an origami rain cloud (grey paper), an origami rock (more grey paper), an origami rock covered in moss (green paper), an origami tent in collapsed form (orange paper) or an origami cricket ball (red paper). If I'm honest, one year this got a little out of hand and, because the children loved it, I had to create a gallery in the classroom where my artwork could be displayed. One child started bringing her own creations from home, my favourite of which was a ball of screwed-up brown paper: an origami potato.

Having a running joke like this definitely has its advantages. It's good to have something that's shared just between you and your children – something that people outside of your classroom don't know about. It brings the class together, strengthens relationships and means that a bit of light relief is never far away when the going gets tough.

The possibilities for showing your playful side are endless, and you're only really limited by your imagination. Tell them you're whatever you like! Using humour and allowing the children to laugh with you, at you, and at each other is not only something they love, but it creates a fantastic climate for learning and makes your classroom a brilliantly positive place to be.

Fallibility

We're not perfect at everything. There'll be things we try in life that we're not very good at, and there won't be a day that goes by when we don't make a mistake.

Making mistakes in front of the children is a good thing. Too many, and you look like an idiot. None, and you're modelling something that's completely unobtainable.

Remember, it takes a smart guy to play dumb!

Along with making mistakes, there should also be a dialogue around struggle. I can remember sitting at school and listening to teachers who gave off an air of knowing everything. For me, the gap was too big – the teachers seemed effortlessly intelligent and gave no hint of the fact that they'd probably worked really hard to get where they were.

We shouldn't be delivering the curriculum from anything even approaching an ivory tower – it's much better to be on the ground getting messy. Fortunately, I don't have to work that hard at making mistakes – it comes pretty naturally. But if you're one of those really bright people, then you're going to have to fake it. When you're modelling writing, don't let it flow easily; let them see you get stuck. If you're asked a question, pretend you don't always know the answer and get them to find out for themselves.

Achieving worthwhile things involves hard work. Along the way, there'll be times when things don't go well, and we make mistakes. We need to build a climate where that is the norm: where learners stick at things, take risks, fail and then try again. And if we're not prepared to do it, then why should they?

Politeness and respect

We're the adults in the room, and if we behave like well-mannered, respectful grown-ups, then it'll soon rub off on our children.

Putting it all together

With all of these traits packed neatly into our ground floor, we're well on the way to creating an all-action guerrilla teacher. However, just before I get on to the teaching side of things, here are some extra tips from my own girls, Eve and Imogen, who – despite both being under ten – are self-confessed experts at identifying the characteristics of truly great guerrilla teachers.

1. Wear stuff that is sensible.

2. Go to the toilet at every break.

3. Teach the children true things.

4. Don't put children on a warning if they're fiddling with something on the carpet (this feels pretty specific – someone's been up to something here).

5. Be strict.

6. Don't be clumsy.

7. Look after the children.

8. Say interesting things.

9. Don't wear your bikini.

10. Don't suck your belly in.

I hope you've got all that.

Chapter 6
BENDING THE RULES

Creative thinking is something teachers in primary schools value pretty highly. It's also something that everyone does. The moment we give a worksheet a miss in favour of another approach, we've used creative thinking – if we picked an activity that really worked and gave it a little twist, we're at it again. It can happen in really small ways, but it's always happening. Being a guerrilla teacher means developing this kind of thinking, and then making sure that the children know we're doing it.

Model it and they will learn

In terms of getting the most from creative thinking, we're already starting from a good place. Nobody wants children to be bored in their lessons, and so we try to make things interesting – we think about ways to make them engaging. We work hard at this because we know it makes a difference. Far more qualified people than me have written at length about what exactly goes on in our brains – and it's thanks to this scientific research that you can say with confidence that children learn better when they're emotionally engaged.

The business of emotional engagement can take many forms, but it's a pretty safe bet that if you walked into a foundation stage or reception class you'd be hard pushed to miss it. In Year 6, you might have to hang around a bit, and certainly avoid the months of March through to about the second week in May.

Beyond Year 6, things seem to tail off even more as it's assumed that, as we grow older, we are much happier to sit and soak up information from those who have all the answers.

When I went to university (I do actually have a degree in this teaching stuff) I found that I frequently had to sit in a lecture hall, in silence, and without moving for up to two hours while 'learning' from someone standing at the front who hadn't been in a real classroom for years. Mine was the first of a brand new primary teaching degree, so before it all began, I was hopeful that things might be done differently.

There's not actually a lot I remember about my course, but the bits that do spring to mind fall into the 'really bad' or the occasionally 'really good' category. In hindsight, I suppose that there's lessons in both. Perhaps they were early guerrillas, subversively modelling bad practice to make us think, 'I'm not doing it like that' – in which case, they were highly effective. For example, following a somewhat unnecessary telling-off from a maths lecturer who never particularly liked me, I learned that you should never put out interesting-looking resources on a table if you expect children (or twenty-year-olds) to pay any attention to what you're saying. (I'd never come across multilink cubes before, and they were a bit of a revelation.)

Among the bad stuff, though, there was one particular shining light. Mr Keith Ayling was a history lecturer. He was nearing the end of his career and, while many of his colleagues sat or stood behind their lecterns, Keith had a very different approach. He was very engaging and had a good sense of humour; he talked with passion about teaching (and occasionally history); he had stock phrases that he used over and over again ('catch the child good' is one that stuck with me). If we got a bit carried away, he settled us down with a squeaky clown's horn. I think he knew that the stuff he was teaching us was neither here nor there. He knew it was the *how* that we really needed. Keith was one of the few creative teachers who taught us. He did things differently because he knew that it made a difference to us.

The challenge is that there is stuff to be taught. All our children must be able to read, write and calculate; across other areas there's other knowledge that's also important. If we can't reach our children emotionally, however, if we don't give them a reason to care, the learning just won't happen.

The traditional model of a didactic teacher is frowned upon in a lot of schools, particularly primary. Didactic teachers are fixed: they set their stall out and let nothing get in the way of the knowledge they need to impart. Their aim is to deliver the curriculum at the children. It's something we've probably all experienced at some point and while I'm generally critical about didactic teaching methods, there's still a big part of me that values a direct teaching approach. It's the bread and butter of what we do, and it's the perfect place to start making the most of our creative thinking skills by taking what we've got and turning it into something amazing.

Chapter 7

LEADING FROM THE FRONT

Step up, guerrillas – it's time for action!

I once came across a colleague who uttered the following memorable phrase: 'I prefer to be a guide from the side rather than the sage on the stage.'

Whether this teacher meant to make themselves unpopular in the staffroom is unclear, but it worked unbelievably well. While there might be a sentiment in there that I can agree with, I'm sick of the battle over teaching methods (and the smugness of people who choose one side or the other). You can be traditional or progressive, employ direct teaching, or facilitate child-led learning. I'm sick of it because it's rubbish. Any teacher worth their salt knows that it's not a matter of choosing one or the other. If you work with children, then you know that there's a place for both, and good teachers alternate, change and adapt their methods according to the situation.

In keeping with this, I'm going to look at the 'sage on the stage' bit first, because in my book (and this *is* my book), there's nothing wrong with leading from the front.

Creative direct teaching: the front line

With the ground floor of our brain busy modelling all of the wonderful aspects of our teacher persona, we can start to head up to the first floor and look at the stuff that does need some thinking about. Teaching.

It's obvious, really; after all, teaching is what we're paid to do. Or at least it *should* be obvious but, recently, things have got a bit blurry. Is it teaching or is it learning? It used to be teaching and learning, then it was learning and teaching. Ofsted used to look at teaching, but now it's learning, and apparently teaching isn't about the teacher teaching any more, it's about teaching and a whole host of other things too.

I've found, recently, that the more I've read about teaching (particularly on Twitter) the more confused I've got, and the more my head's started to spin.

When this happens, the only thing that's kept me sane is reminding myself that most of the people talking about it aren't doing it, and that for all their fancy ideas and references to obscure research, there's no substitute for time spent in a classroom, getting on with it; helping children year on year to reach their potential.

Now, I'm not against reading, and I'm not against research, but when good teachers are having their heads messed with to the extent that they don't know which hoop to jump through next, then something's wrong.

Ofsted have a part to play in this. I'm not going to go on about them, but they have definitely not helped, and over the past few years, teachers have been increasingly unclear about what they're supposed to be doing.

Every teacher wants to be the best they can be and, in schools, we're pressured to move teaching to Ofsted's definition of outstanding. I don't even know what outstanding is any more. I think I used to – but then it became this out-of-control monster making weird statements about 'rapid and sustained progress'.

It took me a while before I realised that I don't actually care. I'm not interested in being outstanding, and I don't think schools should be wasting their time with it either.

I want to be a great teacher – we all do, and while it might sound like just a change of terminology, I think 'outstanding' and 'great' are two very different things. I've seen some really good teachers teach great lessons, and some really good teachers teach awful lessons. In the great lessons, the teachers have relied on their instinct – they know what the children need, and they know how best to achieve it. It's usually simple, clean and straightforward, and there's space for the children to shine.

When it goes wrong, it's often because of thinking too much rather than too little. 'Outstanding' does odd things to us. We've got it all straight in our heads

– simple, clean, straightforward – but then the little voice starts. It might remind us that we should really have more detailed success criteria; it might tell us that we should make sure the more able are working independently from the start; it might laugh at the fact that we've only differentiated a measly four ways; and before long, we're drowning under the weight of all these 'must haves', and our beautiful, clean lesson is a total mess.

The drive for outstanding is oppressive and if schools are genuinely interested in developing teaching – and teachers – then they need to be giving their expert teachers the confidence and freedom to take risks and be brave.

That's what great teaching's about.

Chapter 8

THE FIRST FLOOR: CREATIVE TEACHING, STEP BY STEP

Now that we've dealt with the 'o' word (Ofsted/outstanding – take your pick!), we can get down to the business of being great. In true guerrilla style, we're aiming for a simple, straightforward strategy that has the highest possible impact.

Like I said before, direct teaching is high up on my agenda, even though it seems a very traditional approach. We've already explored how putting teachers out there at the front of the class allows us to model the kind of creative thinking we want our children to develop.

To take this thinking a step further, we're going to look at how we can consciously model this creative thinking through our teaching and the way we deliver our lessons. To take us through this process, we're going to use the handily wheel shaped Guerrilla Guide to Creative Direct Teaching on page 56. I'm not exactly sure what this is: it could be a planning tool, or a prompt. I suppose it's as close as I can get to what's going on in my head when I'm trying to plan creatively.

I'm not trying to claim that this is anything amazingly innovative. This is stuff teachers know and do, day in, day out.

So, step by step, we've got:

1. Decide the outcome.

2. Identify the steps.

3. Review the language.

4. Engage the heart.

5. Check the learning.

6. Troubleshoot and tweak.

The Guerrilla Guide to Direct Teaching

Decide the outcome ...
What knowledge will they have?
What skill(s) will they develop?

Identify the steps ...
Unpick the learning.
How will they get there?

Review the language ...
Make it clear, consistent and repeatable.

Engage the heart ...
What's in it for them?
Why should they care?

Check the learning ...
Use targeted questioning.
Stretch and support.

Troubleshoot and tweak ...
Creative ✓
What could go wrong and what can I do?

Step 1: Decide the outcome

Whenever we look at a piece of learning, we always decide the outcome first. We need to know where we're going before we start thinking about how to get there.

The outcome of any lesson is going to be either knowledge and understanding acquired, or skills developed.

The knowledge and understanding bit used to be straightforward. I started out as a teacher on a diet of pre-written learning objectives. If I wanted to know what to write on my planning sheet, I'd just look in my literacy or numeracy strategy folder and copy it down. For other subjects, I'd go to the QCA schemes of work. I didn't particularly think about it, I just copied it. It's quite possible that since things went a bit prescriptive twenty years ago, we've rarely – if ever – written a learning objective for ourselves. It actually took me quite a few years of teaching to realise that a lot of what I was copying down was total nonsense, and in no way reflected what my children actually needed.

Take English, for example. In the old literacy framework, there were about thirty-three objectives listed under 'Narrative'. By my calculations, it would take 6.6 weeks to teach the whole lot based on a lesson a day. Now, to be fair, we weren't supposed to teach everything in just one unit; we could spread it out a bit over the year – and this is exactly what I did. At the end of the unit, the children would write their story, having spent valuable time learning to 'consider the overall impact of a recorded performance', along with a host of other interesting objectives. I'd take the finished work home to mark, only to find out that it was complete rubbish. It turned out that, while I'd been copying down the objectives that the framework said I should be teaching, I'd missed the fact that my class couldn't form sentences.

Out of the thirty-three objectives, only four were about sentence structure and punctuation. While I don't claim to be an English specialist, this seemed a bit odd to me. If we want children to be effective writers, we should probably spend quite a lot of time on the nuts and bolts – the basics. I want children to write creatively and imaginatively, but not at the expense of writing in clearly formed sentences.

After realising this, I made sure that I deliberately ignored what I was supposed to teach and started making it up on my own. In terms of sentence structure, I probably only use a handful of objectives now – and instead of worrying about covering the whole range, I simply focus on the things that make a difference, and do them over and over again. We work on simple, compound and complex sentences, we work on using a range of punctuation, and we work on spelling. Every unit that I plan has these elements at its core, and while the context might change, the sentence-building skills stay the same.

We are learning to use simple sentences to build tension.

We've got the learning bit up at the front, then the reason or outcome at the end.

We're writing simple sentences so we can build tension in our story.

What are we learning? + Why are we learning it?

We are learning to use compound sentences to add detail.

We are learning to use embedded clauses to describe a character.

If we move on to a different genre, such as journalistic writing, we still need the same kind of sentences, just with a different outcome:

We are learning to use simple sentences to write a caption.

We are learning to use compound sentences to add detail.

(This one stays the same – it's pretty much genre-proof.)

We are learning to use adverbial phrases to add information.

When I got my head around using the learning + outcome building blocks for objectives, I then just played around with the verb in the sentence using Bloom's taxonomy.

I have to admit that if we covered Mr Bloom at university, I must have switched off, because I only remember coming across it after I'd started teaching. If you're not familiar with it, it's a lifesaver if you've always had learning objectives handed to you on a plate.

What it sets out to do is classify learning objectives – or, more accurately, the verbs that can be used to create learning objectives. It starts with Remembering and Understanding and then builds through Applying, Analysing and Evaluating to finish with Creating (in the most recently updated version). While there's a fair bit of criticism out there aimed at Bloom's from some of the intellectual education brigade, this is more to do with it being viewed as a fixed hierachy of skills rather than as a useful bank of words. So, as long as it works for me, and other teachers find it helpful, anyone making snooty comments can get stuffed.

The wheel on page 61 is a simplified version, but I think it's helpful. As a rule of thumb, if it's not on the wheel, I'd think very carefully about what I was doing and why I was doing it.

In the examples above, I've gone for 'Use' which sits in the Applying section. This makes sense to me, as the only way children are going to master sentence structure is by applying their knowledge over and over again. 'Practise' would have been another option from the same section, as would 'Write'.

Even though the objectives are repetitive, don't let this put you off. There's a fair bit of pressure at the moment to show that children are learning something new in every lesson. This seems to have come from Ofsted, who still seem stuck on the idea that children only make progress if they know something, or can do something that they weren't able to do at the start of a lesson.

This is total rubbish. Learning only happens when children have practised something enough to master it, and this only happens when we give them the chance to repeatedly do the things they need to do to improve their work.

Repeat the stuff they need, and ignore the fools that tell you any different!

With the knowledge bit sorted, we can now have a look at the trickier area of skills. Have a look at the example below.

We are learning to cooperate with others

Now this is definitely a skill that we want our children to develop. It's important that they learn to work in groups, but the problem is that it just doesn't happen on its own. You can't just learn to cooperate – it's pointless unless there's something to cooperate over. Using our building blocks from before, we need learning + outcome – you can't (and shouldn't) pull them apart:

We are learning to cooperate with others to perform a scene from *Macbeth*.
Learning (What?) + Outcome (Why?)

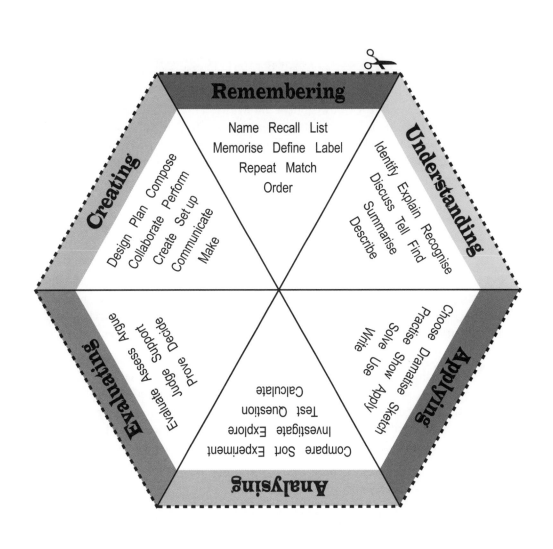

Better, because at least now there's an outcome, but I'm still not happy. I'll talk to the children about cooperation, model it, maybe have prompt cards or specified roles to help them out, but I don't want that to be the point of my lesson. Rather than waste everyone's time, we can get children to develop their collaborative skills in the process of learning something useful.

We are learning to analyse the character of Banquo to perform a scene from *Macbeth*.

We're getting there, but it's now gone a bit wordy. There's nothing worse than a learning objective that doesn't know when to stop. To combat this, and to give the children something shorter to write, repeat or remember, we can cut it down to just the learning bit, and then talk about the outcome or big picture as we're introducing it.

'Today we're going to be performing a scene from *Macbeth*, and to help us get ready for that, we'll be learning to *analyse the character of Banquo.*'

Now we're in business. The children will develop their collaborative skills throughout, but as another layer rather than the main attraction. If the children needed a lot of support with cooperation, I'd make it very structured. If I saw an example of a group doing really well, I'd stop what we were doing and point it out to everyone else.

Skills that are linked to a specific purpose work. We can learn to analyse, evaluate, find, summarise, question or calculate because they relate to content – there's something there to hang it on. The children will develop independence, resourcefulness, resilience, collaboration and whatever else we want because of *how* we structure the learning, not because we've made it the focus of our lesson.

While we're on the subject, here are a few other bits of learning-objective-related advice to help you through what's become a bit of a minefield:

1. Ignore anyone who tells you that you or the children should write down a learning objective in every lesson.

2. Ignore anyone who tells you that you or the children should never write down a learning objective in any lesson.

3. Ignore anyone who tells you that you should always share the learning objective at the start of a lesson.

4. Ignore anyone who tells you that you should never share the learning objective at the start of the lesson.

I think you can see where this is going. Oh, and one last thing: a learning objective is a singular thing. It's on its own, it's clear, it's straightforward. Unless you've got a very, very good reason, don't be tempted to throw in more than one. Keep it simple. Always. Thank you.

Step 2: Identify the steps

When we know where we're going, and we've got a clear outcome, we can start to think about how we're going to get there.

Because of the back-to-front way we work, we're going to have to unpick exactly what the children have to do to be successful in their learning.

It's easy to get drawn into the 'think of an activity' trap. We know what we want, so we find about four differentiated activities that our different ability groups can get on with. Because of this, we often spend more time thinking about what they'll be doing than we do thinking about what they'll be learning.

This is probably a result of the good old three-part lesson thing. When the literacy hour was first launched in schools, there wasn't massive confidence that teachers would get their heads around a lesson in three parts, so a colour-coded clock was produced. There was a twenty-five-minute teacher input bit, then a twenty-five-minute activity section, then finally the all-important ten-minute plenary. All teachers had to do was watch the clock to check which section they were on.

The clock's now long gone, and it looks like the powers-that-be have realised that perhaps teachers have enough intelligence to structure their own lessons without needing to refer to a visual prompt.

You still see remnants of this thinking from time to time, perhaps on a lesson planning sheet (the ones used by some teacher training universities are pretty much always awful) or, worse still, on a lesson observation form.

For the most part, though, we know that the structure of the lesson has to be dictated by the thing that has to be learned.

There'll be times when whatever we want the children to learn fits a three-part structure (although leaving the checking and reflecting bit until right at the end is a bit dodgy) but, equally, there'll be plenty of occasions where it doesn't.

If we've got a big idea, or a tricky concept, then we're better off breaking it down.

Let's take fractions as an example. As an outcome, we might want the children to be able to add fractions using the concept of equivalence, e.g. $2/3 + 5/6$. When I was at school, there would have been a page for that in a maths textbook. There'd be an example in a box at the top of the page, then a page full of sums for me to practise. When I got to the bottom (or if I got stuck), I'd flip to the back, where the answers were, and give myself a whole load of ticks and a smiley face. I was always busy at school, and there were always more pages to complete. Being busy, though, is not the same as learning, and being able to do stuff is not the same as developing a conceptual understanding. Foolishly, when I was choosing A levels, I went for maths and then proceeded to do astonishingly badly, largely due to my lack of understanding of some pretty basic concepts that really should have been ironed out at primary school.

To be successful with this piece of learning, there's a huge amount that needs unpicking.

Do the children remember what a fraction is? (Not just the word 'fraction', but what it actually represents.) Obviously, we'll be building on prior learning here, and we wouldn't be embarking on equivalence if you hadn't worked with them on the basics of fractions first but, as every teacher knows, the effect on the children of having gone home and had a sleep means that nothing can be left to chance!

Following this, how will we get the children to understand the concept of equivalence? Do we want to model it? Have them explore it? Use structured imagery or apparatus? All of the above?

How will we know they've got enough understanding to move on to the concept of addition? How will we check?

How will we get them to see the connection between what they know about equivalence and its usefulness for addition?

How will we simplify the process so they can repeat it for themselves?

How do we want them to be able to justify or explain the process to show their understanding?

How much practice will they need to master this new concept?

With the traditional model, we'd be cramming all of this into the first twenty-five-minute teaching bit before expecting the children to not only remember it all, but to apply it while working through the pre-prepared activity at their tables.

If we've got compliant kids who will just sit, copy off their friends and not make a fuss, we might get away with it. But on a bad day, we'll have a queue of disgruntled nine-year-olds snaking its way around the classroom looking for some one-to-one help because their working memories have only recalled a tiny amount of what we've said. (Think of their brains like a shelf: cram too much on and stuff will start dropping off the edges.)

It's too much to take in, and it doesn't make any sense even to try. Instead, we can build a lesson that contains multiple different parts. We might start by quickly recapping the term 'fraction': 'Turn to your partner. You've got thirty seconds to tell each other what a fraction is, using no more than five words.' Then we can take feedback and check. Next we might go a bit deeper and look at their conceptual understanding of fractions. We could model adding a fraction to a shaded shape, and then have others on the board for the children to try on mini whiteboards: 'You've got three minutes. Try to write the fractions for as many of the shaded shapes as you can.' After this, we might introduce the term 'equivalent'. We'd define it, give a visual representation of what it means, then maybe follow up with another quick activity: 'Using the fraction wall, find three examples of equivalent fractions in three minutes.'

When we've taken feedback, we could show the children how using equivalence can help them to add fractions. We'd model it, maybe using structured imagery, then let them have a go at a couple. After a few minutes, we'd stop, reflect on what we're doing, and have the children explain and justify their thinking:

'What did you notice about the fractions?'

'How did this help?'

'Why did you do that?'

If we were happy with their responses, we might want them to practise some more; if not, we might model more examples.

We're not at the end of the lesson yet, but in this example we've already got a mix of about seven different bite-sized parts. We've avoided the big activity that's more memory challenge than maths and have instead created a session where the children will build the essential steps bit by bit, making sense of and processing the information as they're going along. In other words:

Download …

Process …

Apply …

Repeat.

As you can see from the wavy line graph of learning, these phases don't have to follow a strict sequence, but as a rough guide, if there's an element of teacher input (where the children have to download an instruction or take in a bit of modelling), then it makes sense to follow it up with some form of pupil involvement to give us the best chance of the learning sinking in. If we view this approach across a lesson, we get a lovely wavy line that's a million miles away from the traditional three-part model.

Now before I'm accused of simply upgrading the three-part lesson to a seven-part version, I need you to forget about it. It's in seven parts because it's my lesson, and I needed to break it into seven chunks for it to make sense to me and my children. I'll be teaching English and RE tomorrow, and it'll be different again. Seven is not a magic number, and there are no guerrilla-themed heptagonal coloured clocks. Take every bit of learning on its own merit, pick it apart, and make up your own!

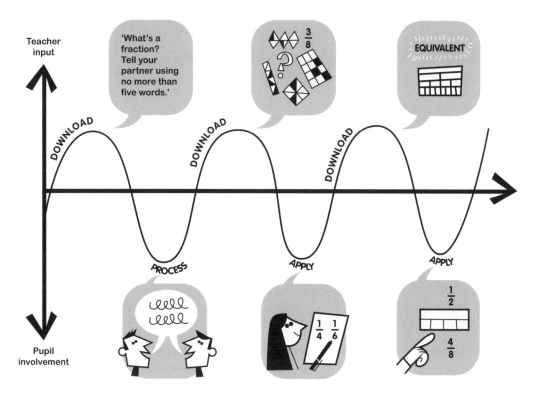

The wavy line graph of learning

Step 3: Review the language

Review the language …

Make it clear, consistent and repeatable.

G

Reviewing the language children use is closely related to the unpicking business we've just looked at. It deserves its own space on the wheel because, the more I think about what makes a great lesson, the more I come back to our use of language.

When I taught in Year 1 at the start of my career, I'd definitely found my level. I was perfectly happy with the kind of language I needed to use to explain number bonds to ten, simple sentences or basic concepts in science. There wasn't any technical language you could throw at me that I didn't understand – I even knew what a phoneme was.

After I had apparently been looking a bit too comfortable for too long, the head teacher (now my sister-in-law – a long story) decided to mix things up a bit and send me up to Year 6.

Initially, this was a bit of a bonus – all of the parents thought I'd been promoted, and I was pretty confident that the older kids would instantly look up to a lively young teacher. It was at this point that everything started to unravel. One of my main problems was that it soon became apparent that I couldn't teach very well. This was a bit of a shock. When you also throw into the mix my inability to get the children to listen, or in fact follow any kind of instruction, it made for a pretty soul-destroying experience. There were many lessons that I'd much rather forget about, including one where an observer from the local authority had to step in and intervene, but one in particular sticks in the memory.

I'd decided that we should do some shape and space work in maths. This decision was made not based on any kind of assessment of what the children might need, but purely because it was a topic I thought I could handle.

After exhausting my knowledge of the properties of 2D shapes we moved on to what I thought was the next logical step: angles. Before the lesson, I was feeling pretty confident. I knew about angles – I'd got a GCSE in maths and I'd been to university. I decided that there was nothing to worry about: I just needed to go for it.

The lesson started well – I had the learning objective on the board and I read it to the children. I'd go so far as to grade this section outstanding. As it turned out, this was probably the highlight of the entire session, and certainly the only point at which I made any sense at all. What I tried to do next was explain what an angle was. I thought I had this. But then I started talking:

'It's the space between two lines.'

'It's the gap where two lines meet.'

'It's where two lines meet at a point.'

'It's where two sides of a shape touch.'

'It can be on the inside of a shape or the outside.'

'If it's 90 degrees, it's a right angle.'

'If it's less than/smaller than 90 degrees, it's acute.' (I used both)

'If it's more than/bigger than/greater than 90 degrees, it's obtuse.' (I used all three)

'If it's bigger than/greater than/goes past 180 degrees, it's a reflex angle.' (again, I used all three)

I also decided to throw in a bit of the classic 'learning about angles arm movements' (think elaborate semaphore) for good measure. The more I talked, the more I got tangled up in a whole host of words that I probably shouldn't have been using, and if the children had even the slightest clue about angles before the lesson, then they didn't by the end.

I thought I knew it, but I didn't. And what I did know, I didn't know with the kind of clarity I needed to teach it. Because it was Year 6, the confusion was obvious to everyone. What it really made me think about, though, was what I'd been doing to those Year 1s. They were too nice to look confused and because they were so eager to please, they'd been putting up with my careless and interchangeable language for quite a while.

It turns out that an angle is a measure of turn.

That's it.

As simple as that.

I know this because I looked it up. I found the definition and I learned it, and now it's burned into my memory.

If I'd have known that, I would have said it. I'd have shown them two strips of card fixed with a paper fastener, moved them, and told them that an angle was a measure of turn. I'd have repeated it throughout the lesson. I'd have got the children to say it to each other, and then back to me. I'd have talked about how we measure the angle of turn using degrees. They'd have nodded, and with total clarity, practised measuring with a protractor while repeating the mantra that an angle is a measure of turn.

At the end of the lesson, I'd have got them to tell me what an angle was and show me how to measure it. I'd have written on a piece of card in black marker[1] that an angle is a measure of turn, and I'd have stuck it onto the side of my board as a permanent reminder of this beautifully simple piece of learning.

This is what should have happened. It should have been clear, it should have been consistent, and it should have been repeatable.

From time to time in newspapers, they use those things called word clouds or wordles. It tends to be when someone important has made a speech and word clouds are used as a quick visualisation of the stand-out points. The bigger the word in the word cloud, the more frequently it was used in the speech. If someone took a transcript of your lesson and turned it into one of these, what would it look like? What would you want it to look like?

---

1 It'll become clear later on why I've got a problem with laminating, but since I've brought it up, I don't think there's anything to beat offcuts of coloured card and marker pens. Why waste your life typing, printing and covering things with shiny clear plastic when you can write it down and stick it up within seconds? Keep a stock of card at the front of the class and you're good to go.

Would it be like my first attempt at angles?

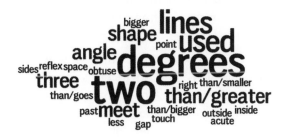

Or would it be more like this:

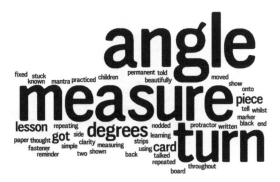

It turned out that it wasn't just angles that I had to learn about. And the more I thought about the words that came out of my mouth, the more I realised that even the simplest of concepts, the stuff that I felt I knew a lot about, could easily be lost under the weight of unnecessary, or inconsistent, language.

Fortunately, instead of making our lives more difficult, it simplifies things.

If we go back to the fractions lesson from earlier – the seven-part one I told you to forget about – there were important bits of language dotted all the way through it.

Look at this: 'Turn to your partner. You've got thirty seconds to tell each other what a fraction is, using no more than five words.' It'd be daft to dish out an instruction like this without having thought about exactly what to say. It's highly likely that we'd already used a particular pre-planned phrase the lesson before, in which case we'd have repeated it enough times for this to sink in, meaning the responses that we'd get from the children today when we recap are going to be accurate, concise and consistent.

What is a fraction? A fraction is a part of one.[2] How will we remember this? Because it's written on a piece of card in black marker pen along with an instantly recognisable image and stuck on the same bit of wall where the angle card is. Another bit of language from the fraction lesson is 'equivalent', and again, we're not leaving this to chance. The definition of equivalent is 'a fraction that can be written in different ways and still mean the same thing'. If we boil this down, we can retain the key meaning but wrap it up in a sound bite that's likely to stick.

What does equivalent mean?

'Looks different, means the same.'

Simple, repeatable and memorable.

Black marker time. Stick it up. Repeat.

---

2 I used to think a fraction was 'a part of a whole' until I read *Primary Maths* by the brilliant Nick Tiley-Nunn. Nick argues that using 'whole' causes problems further down the line when learning about mixed numbers: after all, we say 'one and a half', not 'whole and a half'. This makes sense when you think about it, and also proves beyond all doubt that getting the language right from the start really, really matters.

Step 4: Engage the heart

Engage the heart...

What's in it for them? Why should they care?

I'm sure you remember, but a bit earlier on, we set out to become guerrilla teachers by developing our creative thinking. It won't have escaped your notice, though, that the first three sections of the wheel have gone a bit serious. Decide the outcome, Identify the steps and Review the language are all pretty un-creative and straightforward.

While I'm a massive fan of creativity, I'm also a fan of doing things properly. I think it was Lord David Puttnam who said, 'Creativity without rigour is crap.'

We've got to have the right foundations, because our business is learning, and if we don't get that right, then we may as well pack up and go home. So with learning always taking the front seat, we can safely get on with developing our creative side to make sure that we're engaging the heart. Don't quote me on this, but I think there are three different types of learning that we have to deal with in schools:

● intrinsically engaging learning

● repetitive learning

● dull but important learning.

The top one, intrinsically engaging learning, is pretty much taken care of for us. In most primary schools, if you strolled into any classroom and announced that this afternoon, the children will be doing art, you're likely to get an overwhelmingly positive response. It's the stuff that children just love to do without much, if any, effort from us. You don't generally find teachers tinkering around with art lessons in the same way that you would with fractions – it doesn't need it, and we can leave it as it is.

The most powerful example of this I've ever seen came when I was on teaching practice at a tough inner-city school in Sheffield. My placement was in a reception class with five-year-olds and I was perfectly happy with that. The bigger ones at the other end of the school had a bit of a reputation and, I'd decided, were probably best avoided.

One Friday towards the end of my time there, the head teacher decided that it would do me good to experience some other year groups, and so helpfully arranged a stint with the Year 6s. Fortunately, I was only going to watch, and would be at all times alongside my minder, the unflappable Year 6 teacher.

Sadly, you don't get many teachers like her any more. She was a bit New Age, and seemed to drift serenely around the building with no effort at all. On this particular Friday, it had been raining all day, and the children had been cooped up since arriving at school. The lunchtime supervisors (who were called dinner ladies at the time) had done their best to wind up the class through a combination of shouting at them and giving them incomprehensible instructions. Having taken them to the toilets, they were then attempting to shepherd them into some kind of holding pen as the teacher arrived.

Ignoring complaints from the children about their mistreatment by the dinner ladies, the teacher drifted into the classroom, where the chairs had been set out in a large circle with one chair placed alone in the middle.

As the class came in, they were directed to the chairs that formed the circle. The teacher then floated into the middle and sat down.

What happened next was incredible. She just sat there. Perfectly still, and did nothing, while the children picked up their sketchbooks and drew her. This lasted for forty-five minutes. Forty-five minutes with young people who took pleasure in seeing supply teachers cry.

There's a big part of this that is down to the class teacher's unbelievable relationship with them (she had all of those under-the-surface qualities of a great guerrilla), but it's also an example of a lesson that those children found massively intrinsically engaging and, because of this, just got on and did it.

To this day, it's not something I've tried. I suppose I'm still waiting for the right Friday afternoon, or maybe the next time Ofsted comes in. Let's see them try to grade that!

Now, obviously, if all learning were like this we'd have the easiest job in the world. Sadly, this isn't the case and our challenge is to take the repetitive learning, and all of the dull bits of the curriculum, and turn them into something that's just as absorbing and motivating as the intrinsically engaging stuff.

Repetitive learning

To start this process we'll have a look at repetitive learning – which, if we're honest, is a bit of a headache because as soon as you have to do something over and over again, then there's a good chance that it'll become boring. Unfortunately, there's a lot in school that falls into this category – times tables, for example, are a classic. The children need to know them, and the best way for them to remember them is to practise again and again and again. You could also add number bonds, phonics, spelling and keywords to the list. It's the day in, day out bits that we can't shy away from – but we also can't afford for the children to switch off and lose interest.

Creative thinkers ...
Generate and adapt ideas
Make connections
Be curious   Stick at it
Try things out
Overcome barriers
Challenge your
thinking

If we look back at the Creative thinkers section on the Learning and Thinking Skills wheel, it contains statements like 'generate and adapt ideas' and 'try things out'. This is exactly what we do when faced with turning something potentially boring into something fantastic.

Take practising times tables or number bonds. We'll all have a range of different ways to do it, and we'll have generated these with the sole intention of keeping things interesting.

The ability to generate different ideas is called divergent thinking. The classic test that's often given as an example is the question about how many different uses you can find for a paperclip. While busy guerrillas haven't got time to waste jibber-jabbering about paperclips, thinking up different ways to practise the seven times table would definitely be time well spent.

Have a look at the objects below. How could each of them be used to help children count in sevens? (Or, for that matter, any number you like.)

Marbles

Conkers

A ukulele

A sock puppet

An egg timer

A wooden spoon

A Frisbee

Chalk

A flower

A paperclip (maybe they are useful after all)

A work experience student (see above).

If you're struggling to come up with ideas, ask your children. Give them an object, sit back and see what happens.

One of my current favourites (and the children's – it's not all about me), is my Incredible Swinging Ball™. It's called the Incredible Swinging Ball because despite its apparent simplicity, it has a proven track record of mesmerising children and adults alike. The instructions on page 78 should provide you with everything you need to make your very own device, but basically, what you're after is a tennis ball version of a conker on a string. When you've knocked up your own model, hold the string (or shoelace if you're a bit flash) at the top with one hand at about head height, and the ball will dangle invitingly in front of you. Give the ball a push to the left and it will start to swing like a pendulum, left, right, left right, left right, parallel to your body. That's it. There's nothing more to it. It just swings. How quickly it swings will depend on the length of the shoelace (more on this in a bit), but basically, if you've kept up so far, then you've pretty much mastered the technique needed for this amazing bit of kit. Now, you'd be forgiven for wondering how this simple device might ever engage children, but that's because you haven't had the build-up. In keeping with the 'big it up' advice from earlier, the way that we introduce it to the children will make all the difference.

With a totally straight face, I produce the Incredible Swinging Ball and tell the children that it does something absolutely amazing. (If you really want to go to town on this, you could have it sitting on some kind of pedestal covered by a cloth before whipping it off to reveal the ball underneath!)

When the required amount of anticipation has built up (don't rush this), I ask if they'd be interested in seeing the Incredible Swinging Ball in action. Unsurprisingly, the children are always up for this, so after checking several times that they are really, really ready, I push the ball to the left so that it begins its gentle swing from side to side. After a few swings, when the excitement is almost too much to take, I tend to stop the ball, bow deeply and accept the inevitable applause. After dismissing any children who seem unimpressed by my demonstration, I go on to explain the amazing functionality of my newest invention. Namely, its ability to help us with counting.

The basics

Release the ball and let it swing. Starting with the first multiple, count aloud when it reaches the edge of its arc on the left, then the next multiple as it reaches the edge of the arc on the right. Repeat until you've arrived at whichever multiple you're going up to. It might sound complicated, but with a bit of practice, even a novice guerrilla will pick it up in next to no time.

For whatever reason, this is really popular with the children. One year, I had a parent ask me about it because their child had put it on their Christmas list!

To me, the best thing about it is its adaptability. With the best will in the world, we can't keep generating new idea after new idea. Thinking divergently about the seven times table is great, but we can't let it take up all our time – there's other stuff to be getting on with. Thankfully, creative thinking is just as much about adapting what we've already got as it is about creating something new.

The Incredible Swinging Ball™

What you will need: Ball, shoelace, sharp pokey stick, tape. 	**Step 1:** Take ball and sharp pokey stick. Push sharp pokey stick through ball avoiding hand and any other appendages. 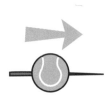
Step 2: Fasten shoelace to blunt end of sharp pokey stick with tape. 	**Step 3:** Take sharp pokey stick and push all the way through ball – shoelace will follow. 
Step 4: Remove tape and shoelace from sharp pokey stick. Tie knot in shoelace to avoid embarrassment of ball dropping off end during use. 	**Step 5:** Your new incredible Incredible Swinging Ball™ is now ready to use.  Happy swinging!

It seems to me that children are relatively easy to fool. Sometimes, all we need to do is give an old favourite a little tweak, and all of a sudden it's as if it's been transformed into something unrecognisably interesting:

Top five twists on the Incredible Swinging Ball

1. Alternate counting: Instead of counting aloud on both sides of the swing, just try it on one – the other side you count in your head. As an alternative you could whisper on one side, and shout on the other. To make things a bit more awkward, try whispering, and then shouting every third/fourth/fifth multiple.

2. Stop/start: To be honest, it's not so much starting as never getting going. Just as the children are primed and ready to count, you can throw in a bit of hesitation. 'OK, are you ready? Here we go … this time … starting on seven … wait for me … here we go … remember it's seven … this side … in a second … here it comes … on your marks … right about now … and … sssss – every time we do this my arm really aches – I can't tell you how hard it is being a teacher!'

    If you really push it, you can take up your entire mental and oral slot without having counted anything – obviously not an everyday strategy, as the children have to learn their tables at some point, but it never fails to get the room buzzing!

3. Accents: You can't beat an accent to spice things up a bit. My current favourites are a posh accent ('Ohhh, one does enjoy the multiples of seven'), Cockney ('You're 'avin' a larff, ain't ya?'), Australian ('No worries, mate'), and the best of all, Geordie ('Why aye, that's proper mint'). If you really fancy a challenge, count in Geordie on one side and Cockney on the other.

4. Speed challenge: A straightforward race against the ball. 'The shorter the string, the quicker it … SWINGS' (this is very definitely 'swings' and not 'goes', as most people seem to think when shouting it back for the first time). As the catchphrase states, the shorter we make the string, the quicker the ball will get, and while there is no real benefit in being able to count at high speed, children do love a challenge!

On my Swinging Ball, I've got small bits of adhesive tack stuck in various positions along the string. These all represent speed challenges: 'Let's speed up a bit and see if we can get to the first/second/third marker.' Somewhat cruelly, there's a piece of adhesive tack barely a centimetre above the ball which, I tell the children, is where last year's class got to. Invariably it's a lie, but you've got to give them something to aim at!

There's something about challenge and competition that engages most children. Without getting all technical, it's down to reward, and anticipation of reward, increasing the levels of dopamine in the brain. I suppose at least this goes some way to explaining why children never seem to get bored with bingo.

5. Magic: What about a bit of magic that would allow you to stop the ball mid-swing and have it suspended, defying gravity, at the edge of the arc? If you straightened out a metal coat hanger, cut it to the same length of the shoelace and then painted it to match, it could then be attached to an identical ball so that it looked indistinguishable from the original. You'd start counting with the normal Swinging Ball, then have to use a bit of misdirection to make the switch. With the fake in place, you'd hold it as if it were the original, make it swing, then make it stop when it reached the edge of the arc so that it was suspended in mid-air. You'd have to switch it back to keep up the illusion, and you might only be able to use it once, but it would be worth it just for the look on their faces.

Beyond this, there will be countless other little creative adaptations that bring a bit of freshness to something that would otherwise become stale. You could have a whole week out of the Swinging Ball, and it'll be something the children will ask for over and over again. One of the reasons why the Swinging Ball is so popular is that it provides an opportunity to apply some of the most effective bits of incidental nonsense around. These examples of quick-fire engagement have a whole host of different applications, and as 'trying things out' ranks pretty high on the creative thinking list, it's worth looking at how some of these techniques and a couple of other strategies might help us to keep engagement levels high.

Use of voice

Anytime, any lesson. Maybe it's not surprising, but from a child's point of view there's nothing better than being given the opportunity to have a good shout. In order to keep some semblance of control, and to channel their passion for noise into something useful, we can focus their energy on particular bits of learning. It might be keywords in science or geography, factors of twenty, or punctuation, it gets their attention and it gets them involved. Try to get the children shouting obscure keywords from a science investigation or a geography topic loudly enough to confuse the teacher next door – just make sure you don't use this strategy when delivering sex education.

For us, it's more about variety. There are times when we use our 'no nonsense, I'm being assertive' voice; at other times it's the 'I'm really passionate about this' voice. There'll be times when we use our cross or disappointed voice, but there shouldn't be many times when we use a shouty one. I'm not a fan of shouting, although there are occasions when I use a loud voice. When it happens, it's always a deliberate choice (rather than losing it!) and is usually when someone's about to come to harm. Shouting isn't a strategy, and while it might work to begin with, its impact soon rubs off and then you're stuffed. I've always had more luck with the opposite end of the spectrum – the surprisingly multifunctional low, quiet voice. First of all, when dealing with bad stuff, the quiet disappointed tone has much more impact than the full-on rant, and is much easier on the vocal cords. More importantly, though, as a tool for engagement, there's nothing better than a sudden drop in volume to draw children into the moment. They physically move forward and listen more intently to make sure that they're not missing anything … and in an instant, the atmosphere in the classroom is transformed. Sshhhhh.

Anticipation

I'll tell you about this a bit later. (Sorry – couldn't resist!)

If you use the hesitation trick to build anticipation with the Swinging Ball, you'll find that it's addictive and you won't be able to stop yourself from transferring it to other areas. Try hiding or covering a key piece of information or a sound bite on the board, then having a drum roll before letting the children see it. (Breaking off the drum roll a couple of times to clarify that they understand the instruction really drives children mad.)

Another strategy related to this is something called *throwing forward*. I first came across this in a brilliant book called *Essential Motivation in the Classroom* by Ian Gilbert (a true guerrilla educationalist if ever I've seen one). The technique is widely used in television and radio and is intended to keep an audience listening by dropping out bits of information about what's coming up next. In the classroom, we can make the most of this by following a similar script:

'We're going to do a quick activity now, and in five minutes, I'm going to tell you something amazing.'

Or

'Coming up after playtime we'll be looking at something you've never seen before.'

Admit it: you want to know what it is.

Props

The Swinging Ball, for all its impressiveness, is ultimately just a prop. And for the guerrilla teacher, it's just one of many that are constantly within easy reach:

Inflatables

Hammers, bananas, microphones, dinosaurs – you name it, and there'll be an inflatable version. Just like the inside of a well-organised garage with all the tools carefully positioned on the wall, make yourself an inflatable prop wall so they're all accessible at a moment's notice. When we were talking about learning objectives earlier, we looked at sentence structure as an example. Because we're aiming to practise the same things over and over again, why not spice things up with a bit of inflatable action? If you're building a sentence, have the children out at the front holding the word cards, then take your inflatable hammer and bash out the sentence, hitting each child on the head in turn. The following day, you could take down the inflatable tennis rackets and kick off with a game of adverb tennis, with one child hitting verbs, and the other firing back adverbs until the victor wins the inflatable trophy. How about using the inflatable sword to chop sentences into clauses? Or the inflatable dice to generate numbers for calculations in maths? Even the briefest of searches on the Internet will bring up hundreds of blow-up items that can be used (as well as a few that you should probably leave well alone).

Novelty glasses

Why these aren't provided as part of teacher training is beyond me. Buy a selection – the more the better! You never know when you'll need them. If you've already got the glasses, try branching out into novelty eyebrows. Cut out the selection on page 84 and glue firmly to your face.

Honkers, bells, squeakers and other noisy stuff

My university lecturer used the squeaky clown's horn, and it was thanks to him that I started my own collection of noisy props. They can be used to signify things, like time to stop, or time to start. They could highlight a great answer or draw attention to the most important part of the lesson (try using a megaphone for this – if the children don't pay attention after that, they never will). Another favourite is the use of sound effects or clips. Again, if you search for sound clips, there are hundreds of brilliant noises up for grabs: maybe you could use something like 'evil laugh 2' when a child comes up with something diabolically clever ('evil laugh 1' didn't quite do it), or 'ovation' if the class has done something incredible. Most of them are pretty general, although there are some strangely specific ones out there, such as 'night rain in Russian city' or 'alpaca mating call'.

Having a range of options is always a good thing, but I tend to settle on one way of signalling that I want the children's attention, and then I stick with it so it becomes a ritual. The idea of noisiness also plays a part in my all-time favourite behaviour management system: marbles.

I've already talked about the horrible time I had when I was moved from Year 1 to Year 6. Along with not knowing what I was talking about, the other problem

The Mad Scientist

The Evil Supervillain

The Classic Monobrow

I had was that I couldn't control them. When I got the class, part way through the autumn term, they were climbing the walls, and not in the slightest bit interested in listening to some inexperienced young teacher. The only thing that saved me was marbles.

The children were in their own groups and had been allowed by the previous teacher to make up their own group names. After ditching this for my preferred seating plan and then dishing out group names that I could actually remember (Amazing, Fantastic, Terrific, Outstanding and Sensational groups), I set about taking advantage of the children's competitiveness in a desperate attempt to tame them.

Each group had an empty pot in which they were going to collect marbles. I controlled the pots, and had them on a table at the front of the classroom. At the end of a half term, the group with the most marbles won the highly desired table prize. The prize was usually in chocolate form, and while I'm all for healthy eating, I wasn't prepared to overlook the single most effective means of bribing children known to mankind.

Marbles were gained by following school rules, showing positive behaviour, having a positive attitude to learning and being generally kind and lovely to their teacher. It worked a treat – the children desperately wanted to have the most marbles and responded brilliantly. Before long, they were reminding each other about their behaviour, just so they were in with a chance of a couple of extra marbles in their pot. I found that, after a while, I didn't need to tell them to be quiet or to stop; I just shook my pot of marbles and the room fell silent. The marble shaking sound became my stop signal, and I was finally in a position to get on with teaching. Now, I don't want to get bogged down with the rights and wrongs of intrinsic/extrinsic motivation, but sometimes you need a strategy that will get a challenging group of children responding quickly. In an ideal world, the learning that the children are doing would be motivation enough to behave, but sometimes you need a strategy that will give you a chance and, for me, the marbles worked a treat.

Since then, I've used the marbles with every year group I've taught in one way or another. Sometimes they'll have pots for each group, while at other times I've used a class pot. I've come across countless different systems for encouraging and rewarding positive behaviour but haven't found any that are as easy to use as this.

With a handful of marbles in a pocket, you don't even have to break stride in your teaching – just whip them out, give them a shake and drop in a pot.

Hats and headdresses

A bit like the novelty glasses – get hold of some and stick them in your prop box.

Here's a rundown of my favourites:

1. A builder's hat (great for the sentence building we talked about earlier or for a quick warm-up in maths – three children wearing three hats, with three different digits stuck on the front: how many different calculations can you write down in three minutes?).

2. A crown (could be used for a 'star of the day', or worn by any of your children who have done something brilliant. Failing that, wear it yourself and make the children call you 'Your Majesty').

3. Kung fu-style headbands (I first came across kung fu punctuation when watching Phil Beadle on the TV show *The Unteachables*. Along with frequently doing all the actions, we also knocked up a set of black headbands for them to tie round their heads to remind them all to use a full range of punctuation whenever they did a piece of writing. They liked them so much, they wore them in their SATs writing test!).

4. A wizard's hat (if you can get one with a hidden compartment inside, as well as wearing it, you can also use it to magically produce all sorts of useful things!).

5. A sombrero (not that great for the classroom, but will keep you nice and dry on a rainy playground duty).

Puppets

I've always used puppets with younger children, and it's always gone well. It took me a while, though, to summon up the confidence to give it a go with streetwise eleven-year-olds, as I thought they'd be a much more cynical crowd. My first foray into the world of puppets was pretty low-key. I decided I'd start by building up characters using a bit of personification. I thought if I got the children used to me talking to inanimate objects, then they'd be much more willing to go along with things when I started to make them talk back. An obvious choice seemed to be the classroom plants. If you haven't got at least a couple of plants, then get some – they brighten things up, and they're much less irritating than a class hamster.

When you've got them, get hold of some of those self-adhesive googly eyes and stick a pair on one of the leaves. When they're looking the part, give them a name or, better still, set up a competition for the children to name them. With names sorted, they quickly become part of the class – and as a result, should be included in the register so they don't feel left out. It's amazing how quickly even the most streetwise of children will buy into this bit of nonsense. It takes us back to the idea of modelling playfulness, and I find it massively reassuring that even with all the pressure that's piled on our young people to grow up, when given the chance, they can't wait to play along and join in with the daftness.

So with Betty, Bernard and Taloolah firmly installed as our perennial classmates, it was time to give it a whirl with a proper puppet. I first came across Brian in a garden centre. He's a monster with red and black fur, and he's got a hole up his back so you can operate his oversized

gawping mouth. I'd decided that Brian was perfect for livening up a potentially boringly repetitive lesson on number facts.

With Brian hiding away in my prop box off to the side of the classroom, I told the children that I had a very special friend I wanted them to meet. Thanks to the plant antics, there were pretty high levels of anticipation as they sensed that something stupid was about to happen. After a good amount of hesitation (triple-checking that they were definitely, absolutely sure they wanted to meet him) Brian emerged from his box to a hero's welcome. To be honest, it all got a bit too much and things got a bit emotional, but after recovering, Brian was able to tell the children, via whispering in my ear, that he had come to help them with their maths lesson because he was, in fact, a maths genius. Brian went on to explain that he could work out any maths problem that they could think of at incredible speed. To demonstrate, he encouraged the children to think up and then ask some questions. When the questions started flying, Brian went into maths genius mode and dealt with them all, every time answering with the number seven. Before long a couple of the more unruly Year 6s started to doubt his ability and throw a bit of criticism his way. Inevitably, this upset Brian and he retreated sadly back to his box. We decided that Brian wasn't a genius after all, but to cheer him up, we should make him feel like one. This meant somehow cleverly devising a range of different questions where the answer was always seven. What followed was a fairly standard 'how many different ways can you make seven?' type lesson, but the focus and determination brought about by the children's engagement was incredible. They didn't think he was real, but they loved playing along, and it had a hugely positive effect on their learning.

My only real problem was that I hadn't anticipated just how much the children would like him. What started out as a quick-fix means of engaging children in a maths lesson snowballed into them insisting that Brian be part of more of our lessons. At the start, I'd been nervous about even using a puppet, and then it turns out that he was even more popular than me. Brilliant.

Fancy dress

I love a bit of dressing up. Quite often, it's not a full-on costume, maybe just a piece of clothing that either lets the children know that something different is happening, or signals that I've stepped into role (there's more about this on page 123). When we're doing science investigations, I put on a lab coat (always two sizes too small, for comic effect). Along with the entertainment value, there's a message in there too: we're not just doing a science lesson, we're being scientists. In an ideal world, all the children would have one too, but as this is a bit of a luxury, I've always made do by having my coat make the rounds. If a child is feeding back results to the class, they wear the coat (and possibly the 'mad professor' eyebrows too if they're up for it). If you can get your hands on a few child-sized coats, you could set up your own mini team of scientists. Whenever you do an investigation, you gather a small group of children (chosen based on attitude and behaviour in the last science session) to be the scientific research team. Give them the coats, a clipboard each and arm them with a couple of key questions or things to look out for. When briefed, set them the task of monitoring and supporting the other children while they carry out their investigations.

Some of the fancy dress isn't fancy at all. If you're teaching a PE lesson, wear PE kit (this doesn't mean an old school vest and pants, just something sporty to let the class know just by looking at you that you value physical activity). If it's art, throw on one of your dad's old shirts; in a dance lesson, wear a tutu. Whatever it is you're doing, if you look the part, you'll act the part – and so will the children.

Movement

People who are engaging tend to move around. Not in a manic, non-stop, pacing, desperate for the toilet kind of way, but in a way that means it's hard for you to take your eyes off them. Sometimes the movement can be very slight, like a tilt of the head, a raising of the eyebrows or a moment of very deliberate stillness. At other times it might be more exaggerated. Lots of teachers, for example, use their hands while talking to illustrate their points in mid-air – in fact, it's virtually impossible not to. (If you ever go out with other teachers to a restaurant, watch them ordering food or asking for something – they can't help themselves!)

If space in your classroom allows it, make sure you give yourself room to move around at the front. It's easy to get stuck next to the interactive whiteboard, but regardless of how pretty your flipchart or PowerPoint pages are, expecting the children to maintain focus for an extended period on one fixed point is never going to happen. If you think about the way we broke down the learning when we looked at Step 2: Identify the steps, we'll have natural opportunities to move to the board to model something, then back closer to the children to give instructions to practise. You can also throw in the use of keywords to add movement to Review the language (Step 3). If we're talking about a simple sentence, we could signal the subject with an outstretched right hand, the verb with an outstretched left hand, and a simple sentence by bringing both hands together. The first time, model the language along with the movement:

'In a simple sentence we have a *subject* [right hand] and a *verb* [left hand] … a simple sentence has one *main clause* [both hands brought together].'

Although these are made-up actions, you could also try searching on YouTube for clips of sign language, or use a website like www.spreadthesign.com where you can search for the specific words you're after. Signs for maths are pretty easy to come by, and often give not just an action, but also memorable imagery that goes some way to explaining the concept you're after. If we want to sign 'add' or 'addition', for example, we use both hands with fingers open in a grabbing position, and bring them together to symbolise gathering digits from different columns. An 'angle' is another nice simple one – if only I'd checked at the time!

When we've done the actions and said the words, we can write them on some of your bits of card, move to the side of the classroom, and stick them on the wall. When we revisit the learning, feed the children the cues, and have them fill in the gaps by referring to the word cards on the wall:

'In a simple sentence we have a _____ [right hand], and a _____ [left hand] … a simple sentence has one _____ [both hands together].'

With enough practice (whisper, shout, Geordie and posh) we'll be able to cover the words on the wall, and the children will be able to remember the lot just by doing the actions. Having a particular place near the front where you always place your keywords is a useful technique. At the right-hand side of my classroom is a stand-up flipchart. This is the place we go to read keywords. They'll be stuck on there, and whenever we're ready to repeat them during the lesson, I'll head over, point, and we'll read them together. When we've moved on to a different topic or lesson, the word cards migrate to the wall behind so they're still easy to refer to. Having them in one spot also throws up another unexpected advantage. During SATs, you have to cover up anything that might help the children so the SATs police don't arrest you for cheating. After doing this using impenetrable black fabric, I noticed that lots of the children were staring at the sheets as if there was something useful written on them. After the test, I pulled a couple of them aside to double-check they didn't have some kind of superior vision, and they told me that they were looking at the wall because they could remember where different words and definitions were. They'd inadvertently developed a brilliantly useful visual memory thanks to us repeatedly going over language that was in a specific place in the classroom. It didn't matter that it was covered up; they could still 'see' it, and then use it to help with their test.

Along with a keyword corner, having a telling-off spot is also a useful trick. Sometimes we need to deliver a whole class talking-to about some terrible crime, such as messing about in the cloakroom. One of the problems with doing this centre stage is that, as soon as we've finished pointing out their failings, we've got to switch into 'nice teacher' mode to get on with whatever's up next. To make this transition easier, we can move our telling-off position. In my classroom, it's off to one side, and is called the 'summat's up' spot thanks to one young man who realised pretty quickly what it was for. Regardless of where it is, when you've delivered your telling-off, you can physically move back to the front, by which time, they've got the message that the telling-off is over; we're back to normal and ready to move on. Keep this up and, before long, you'll only have to move into your 'summat's up' position before they get a sniff that trouble's brewing. (If you're really cross, go for the classic 'serious face and raised eyebrows' look, and you'll put a stop to whatever nonsense they were up to in seconds.)

Used in the right way, movement and actions bring just the right amount of variety to our teaching. We become more interesting to look at, and the children respond by looking and listening closely. If you can bear it, buy yourself a mini tripod; attach your smartphone and film yourself delivering a lesson. It's horrible, but you'll see immediately whether you're buzzing around like a demented Pac-Man, or resolutely rooted to the spot.

Competition

For lots of children, all it takes is the slightest whiff of a challenge, and they're hooked. Like the bits of adhesive tack on the Swinging Ball, or throwing in a timed challenge ('How many adjectives can you find in sixty seconds?'), introducing an element of competition really seems to do the trick. Handily for us busy teachers, there's also a bunch of old favourites that never fail to go down a storm.

The top five most popular games (according to my class!)

1. **Bingo** (I told you!): it seems that any kind of bingo will do (times tables, keyword bingo) – as long as they get to shout 'Line' or 'House' they're happy.

2. **Adverb tennis** (as described earlier).

3. **Winking murder**: this classic combines whodunnit-style tension, creativity and the opportunity for children to murder their peers in a friendly, safe

environment. Have the children sit in a circle (either on chairs or on the floor) and select a detective. Give them a deerstalker and Sherlock Holmes-style pipe from the prop box and send them out of the room to get into character. With the detective out of the way, get the rest of the children to put their heads down and close their eyes so that you can anonymously select the murderer. If you've been having a bad day, now's the time to nip out for a quick cuppa – the anticipation of waiting to see if they will be the chosen one means the class will stay pretty much motionless for a surprising amount of time. When you've made them wait long enough, tap one eager homicidal maniac on the shoulder and have all the children lift up their heads so they're ready to begin. At this point, it's really important that the chosen killer does not reveal their identity to anyone else in the room, and especially not the detective when they're invited back into the circle to attempt to solve the crime. The game begins with the murderer trying to knock off victims with a sly wink, while at the same time attempting to avoid being collared by the detective. Added tension is heaped on our super sleuth by limiting them to just three attempts at correctly guessing the identity of the murderer. If they guess correctly, they win; if not, then the murderer gets away with it and, if they so wish, can choose to be the detective in the next round.

As it stands, this is a pretty entertaining way to while away a few spare minutes, but the game comes into its own when there's a bit of effort and creative thought put into how the victims meet their untimely demise. If you're winked at, then you have to die: there's no two ways about it, you're a goner. However, if you've got any self-respect at all, then you owe it to yourself to go out with a bang. The minimum required of you as a victim is to say the words, 'I'm dead', but for the imaginative thinkers among us, there are countless over-the-top theatrical exits that can be employed. If you really wanted to up the competitiveness and encourage some truly beautiful 'dying swan' routines, then dipping back into the prop box for a plastic Oscar statue would be all the incentive the children would need.

4. **One line at a time:** like adverb tennis, this is also English-related, but before you dismiss it as being a bit of a boring choice, this is story writing with a difference. Starting with 'Once upon a time', the story builds as you move around the class, with each child adding a new phrase to help move the story along. Admittedly, it's hard to keep any sort of cohesion or

theme, but it never fails to throw up some interesting and very creative ideas. To spice things up a bit, you could pause the game with your special honker and make the child who's next up choose either a mystery object (from your prop box or inflatables collection) or a mystery word (from the ones you've been shouting aloud to unsettle the teacher next door). Whichever they go for, they'd have to somehow weave it into their phrase before the story continues with whoever's next in line. Adding an element of competition to this is pretty easy, but rather than relying on the player who's fastest, this time you can reward the children who make the funniest/most creative/most interesting/most dramatic additions to your tale.

5. **Fizz Buzz**: if you've not come across this one, it's a maths game designed to help practise different division facts. To play the game, the children stand in a circle and take turns to count (usually starting at 1). Whenever they get to a number that's divisible by three, for example, they say 'Fizz', and whenever they get to a number that's divisible by five, they say 'Buzz'. If they get to a number that's divisible by both, they have to say 'Fizz Buzz'. Players who hesitate or make a mistake are out until only the winning player remains. (This works just as well as a drinking game on a staff night out – simply replace the words 'Fizz Buzz' with some completely inappropriate alternatives, and line up the sambucas for the loser.)

Not enough competition for you?

race you to the next page

Being a creative teacher means thinking like a creative teacher, and for repetitive learning to become something the children love rather than switch off from, the more strategies we've got the better. While the ideas we've looked at are tried and tested, they're by no means a comprehensive list and, without thinking too hard, I bet you could reel off a list of your own techniques that work for you with your children. Stuff that makes them smile, keeps them happy and ensures that they're engaged with even the dullest of day-to-day practice.

'Today is gone. Today was fun. Tomorrow is another one.'

Dr Seuss

How will you make tomorrow as fun as today?

Step 5: Check the learning

In terms of engagement, I'll come back to the 'dull but important' learning a little later. Now, let's get back to the creative teaching wheel before I totally lose track of where I've got up to.

So far I've covered the following steps:

Check the learning...
Use targeted questioning.
Stretch and support.

● Decide the outcome

● Identify the steps

● Review the language

● Engage the heart.

Which leads me to the fifth step: Check the learning.

Back in the days of the colour-coded literacy hour clock I mentioned earlier, any kind of checking of learning was withheld until the final ten minutes of the lesson. We'd teach some stuff for twenty-five minutes, have the children practise for twenty-five minutes and then keep our fingers crossed that when we asked them about it in the plenary section, they'd remember it all so we could chalk the lesson up as a success. In reality, we'd probably have a bit of a feel for how the lesson was going as things were ticking along, but just because children are on-task and busy, doesn't necessarily mean they're learning anything. On my planning, and still present on many of the planning sheets that I come across today, the plenary or assessment questions still sit firmly rooted in the far right column of the sheet. For as long as they are there, there's the possibility that they will remain tacked on to the end of your lessons.

In an attempt to change this thinking, the mini-plenary was launched. I say 'launched', but I have no real idea when it started. All of a sudden it seemed that if you weren't adding multiple mini-plenaries to your lessons, you were embarrassingly out of fashion. The thinking behind this was spot on, and anything that helps us to check the learning as it's happening as opposed to when it's finished is a definite improvement.

I'm not really sure why we have to call them plenaries, though, and when I looked up plenary in the dictionary, it made even less sense:

Plenary: adjective: 'describes a meeting at which all the members of a group or organisation are present, especially at a conference.'[3]

It seems to me that if we have to stop our lessons to check that everyone's present, then we're in real trouble. So from this point onwards, safe in the knowledge that most of us know where most of our children are at any given moment, I'll ditch the word 'plenary' (and all its variations), and instead focus on something much more straightforward. Asking questions.

When I looked at identifying the steps in learning, it was clear that the vast majority of direct teaching will come punctuated throughout with several stops and starts. These will happen for different reasons, but each stage gives us the opportunity to assess the learning as we're going along.

The model I used included the following phases: *Download, Process, Apply, Repeat.* These give us the opportunity to plan specific questions that will support each stage of the learning process.

Download

Any questioning at this point is likely to fit into the 'remembering' category. We're teaching the children something, and we can check that it's going in by using questions that assess recall.

'Can you name ...?'

'What is ...?'

'Is that true or false ...?'

'Choose three words from the board and tell your partner what they mean.'

---

3 See http://dictionary.cambridge.org/dictionary/british/plenary.

Sometimes, this assessment doesn't even come in the form of a question – it might be a statement that the children finish off: 'Tell me what equivalence is. Looks different, means the …?'

We could also assess recall without having to say a word. Making use of our handwritten keyword cards that we've stuck at the front, turn a couple over and point. If they can remember it, brilliant; if not, flip it back and try again!

Process

We've built in the process aspect to our learning based on the idea that we can't be in two places at once. We're either focusing on what's being said (taking information in) or trying to make sense of it (processing). Giving the children time to internalise and take on board new information leads us to the next stage of questioning. Beyond simply recalling, what we want here is a signal that they've understood what's been said.

'Can you explain in your own words ...?'

'Why do you think ...?'

'Can you give an example ...?'

'Could you summarise ...?'

'Can you identify the key points ...?'

These kind of questions need to be followed up with the children talking to their partners to give them the time and opportunity to process, share, compare and compose a response. What it also does is avoid the terrible 'rabbit in the headlights' moment of a child being put on the spot when they're still trying to get their head around what the teacher's just said.

We can also dig a little deeper to discover what level of understanding the children have, with a couple of well-placed clarification questions:

'Can you tell me a little bit more about that ...?'

'Could you explain what you mean ...?'

'Can you find another way of saying that ...?'

To keep everyone on their toes, we could also throw things open to other unsuspecting children:

'Do you agree with that?'

'What do you think?'

'Could you add anything to their answer?'

'Could you explain that in a different way?'

One of the biggest advantages of using this approach (and having the children know that it's likely to happen) is that it significantly reduces the amount of switching off that can happen in any given lesson. When we pick the pair to respond, there's a good chance that everyone else in the room will breathe a collective sigh of relief and then miss the answer the chosen ones are giving. If, however, there's the expectation that everyone listens to every response, and this is backed up by the fact that, for any given answer, we could well ask any other pair in the room for an opinion, zoning out and switching off is not something children can afford to do.

Apply

Now that the children have downloaded and processed, they're ready to apply their knowledge by practising. Again, there are some useful question types that take advantage of the fact that whatever piece of learning they're focusing on, the children will now be at the point where it's really starting to make sense to them. As a result, they can cope with a bit of extra thinking thrown their way.

'How could you use this learning to help with ...?'

'How is this linked to/related to ...?'

'What would happen if ...?'

'Tell me how/where/when/why ...?'

'Predict what would happen if ...?'

As with all of these questions, we'll carefully gauge whether it's the right time to throw them into the mix, so we end up with just the right levels of challenge and support. If the response we get from the children is uncertain, we can easily drop down a level to work out exactly what they need:

Scenario A

Pupil: 'I'm stuck.'

Teacher: 'Can you explain the task to me?'

Pupil: 'Yes ...'

(*Pupil has processed the learning, but is unsure how to apply it.*)

Teacher: 'That's fantastic, let's make a start by ...'

(*Teacher models the application, or gives a starting point until pupil is clear.*)

Scenario B

Pupil: 'I'm stuck.'

Teacher: 'Can you explain the task to me?'

Pupil: 'No!' (*Or gives a confused/incorrect explanation.*)

Teacher: 'Can you tell me the first thing we did?'

(*Teacher prompts recall by asking the pupil to remember.*)

Pupil: 'We ...' (*If the pupil remembers, brilliant – we build on it until they are secure on all the necessary elements of the learning. If not, it's back to the drawing board and we teach it again!*)

As well as dropping our levels of questioning, we can also raise them, and for children who have mastered a particular piece of learning, there's nothing better than dropping in some 'wonderings':

'I wonder why ...?'

'I wonder what would happen if ...?'

'I wonder if there's a reason for ...?'

'I wonder if that is always the case ...?'

Wondering questions are arguably not questions at all, but statements that just hang there, waiting to be explored. They're fantastic things to drop into a group, and while in reality we probably already know the answer, the idea of withholding expertise is an important and very handy technique. Besides, no one likes a show-off.

As we're repeating the Download, Process, Apply cycle through the lesson, we'll be moving in and out of the different types of questions as part of the natural flow of the session. In the olden days, we'd tie things up nicely with our ten-minute plenary, and even though the thinking on this has shifted, you still need a proper end to the learning – there's nothing worse than a lesson that just drifts into nothingness.

The ending

Because of the questioning techniques we've used in the lesson, we're totally clear on the learning that's taken place. So rather than waste ten minutes checking again, just for the sake of it, we can use this valuable time at the end of the lesson for something much more important: reflecting and evaluating.

'What is your opinion of ...?'

'How did you feel about ...?'

'Based on what you know, how would you explain ...?'

'How effective was ...?'

'Is there a better way to ...?'

And when we're happy we've got a good range of questions planned that will stretch, support and check the learning, we're almost ready to teach. Almost.

Anyone for a plenary?

No, I didn't think so.

Step 6: Troubleshoot and tweak

We're almost good to go, except for the last little step, Troubleshoot and tweak. We've pretty much got our lesson sorted from start to finish, but there's always the chance that we've done something a bit daft that might potentially trip us up. After all, we're only human. The learning should be completely clear because it was our first port of call, but since then, we've used our first-floor creative thinking to spice things up a bit, and it's this move upstairs that often causes problems.

To illustrate this, I don't think there's a better example than Luigi the pizza chef.

In the previous sections I've been using fractions as an example. I don't know what it is about primary school teachers, but we can't resist the temptation to dress up a bit of maths in some entertaining context.

I've lost count of the different creative approaches I've seen to teaching fractions. I've seen teachers in full-on chef outfits teaching with an Italian accent. I've been in classrooms that have been lovingly transformed into cafes, complete with tablecloths and romantic music. One teacher had chefs' hats for all the pupils and had spent hours printing, laminating and cutting out colourful pizza templates for every group. Now, this might sound great, but at the end of these lessons, while the children could talk happily about their favourite pizza toppings, they were no clearer about fractions than when they'd begun.

All of the teachers had set out with the right intentions: they wanted the children to learn about fractions, and they wanted the lessons to be engaging and fun. There's nothing wrong with this, and it's exactly how guerrilla teachers should behave; it's just that things got a bit back to front.

With our pizza chefs, the thinking looked like this:

Engagement, Activity, Learning

Learning took a back seat, with engagement to the fore.

What it should have looked like was this:

Learning, Activity, Engagement

If we're going to get the most out of our children, then our energy and effort has to be focused in the right area. One of the risks of thinking about learning first, then applying our first-floor creative thinking, is that potentially we can mess things up. We might be delighted with the bits of quick-fire engagement that we've added in, but they're there to enhance the learning, not to get in the way of it. This is a bit of a personal one, and also one to gauge with your class. If these approaches are part and parcel of your daily teaching (which after all is very much a part of your playful teacher persona), then it's highly likely that the children will respond in exactly the right way, with laughter, smiles, and then the focus needed to succeed in their learning.

Along with checking that your attempts at engagement aren't messing things up, troubleshooting also gives you the chance to think about and pre-empt possible misconceptions, potentially tricky bits, or elements of structure and organisation that could cause you problems.

If I give the children this task to do, does it:

- Help them to learn what they need to learn? (as opposed to just keep them busy)

- Throw up any undesirable difficulties that will get in the way of learning? (we'll look at desirable difficulties a bit later on)

- Need careful management because it involves children having to share/take turns/organise or do something else that children frequently need a bit of support with to avoid things descending into chaos?

To help with this, another useful tactic is to swap your teacher's head for a child's head. If you were on the receiving end of your lesson, how would it feel? At which points might you say that 'you don't get it', and what could be done to explain? Where are the bits where you might drift off-task or poke your friend with a pencil? Are there periods where you'd be listening for just a bit too long? Or are there bits that move on too fast?

This process isn't reserved just for the end, and it's highly likely that we've already been busy ironing out issues throughout. It's good to check, but it's also good to remember that there'll be times when things slip through the net and mess with our best-laid plans, regardless of how much we've thought things through. When it happens, we need to put on our bravest face and tell ourselves that we're entitled to teach a rubbish lesson once in a while. Besides, in the words of one of the greatest thinkers of our times, 'I make mistakes [...] I'm not perfect. I'm not a robot.' And if that's good enough for Justin Bieber, it's good enough for us.

Putting it all together: first-floor teaching

With the sections of the wheel sorted, we can start to get to the good bit: putting it all together. My early attempts at creating engaging lessons were interesting, to say the least. At the start of my career, I came across a school in some kind of terrible Ofsted category and, not knowing any better, applied for a job there. After drifting through the interview monosyllabically, I was offered the post and happily set about my first term under the watchful gaze of Her Majesty's Inspectors.

As we were getting ready for the follow-up inspection that was to re-launch us as an institution that no longer did children harm, I started to get a bit twitchy. These days, we forget how lucky we are with the quick in-and-out two-day inspections. In those days, they set up camp for nearly a week. Imagine the stress of having to plan properly for four whole days!

Along with having to plan properly, you also had to plan for virtually every subject under the sun, because you never quite knew when they'd turn up.

As a new teacher, my brain was firmly focused on the ground floor. I was hoping that I would at the very least look and sound a bit like a real teacher and therefore deflect any attention from my teaching. As a result, I decided that simplicity was best. I wanted lessons that were so completely straightforward that nothing could possibly go wrong. While flicking through the Year 1 science curriculum, I came across a bit of learning to do with the parts of a plant. This was exactly the kind of thing I was after. Flower, petal, leaf, stem … I knew it inside out.

My first thoughts were to get hold of a picture of a flower, blow it up on the new fancy colour photocopier, then use it to model the different parts to my expectant class of five-year-olds.

I'd use my pointing stick to highlight the different bits, they'd say the words back, and then I'd send them off to their tables to get on with their jobs. I even intended to keep the inspectors happy by having a bash at differentiation – my more able group would draw their own plant, and then label it for themselves. My middle groups would also draw their own, and then add pre-written labels in the right places. My lower group would do some nice cutting and sticking under heavy supervision from an adult so they didn't eat the glue (again).

Straightforward, simple and couldn't possibly go wrong. Maybe this is where I should have stopped, and maybe it would have been – had it not been for the first floor of my brain slowly whirring into life. The first floor told me that I could do better. It told me that I shouldn't just settle for something boring, that I shouldn't just settle for my first idea. It told me that I should get creative.

The first floor took over.

It began gently, with some cautious what ifs?

What if you used a real flower instead of a picture?

What if you had flowers for the children?

What else might they notice if they could touch, feel, smell the flowers rather than just looking at a picture?

I still liked the idea of them being able to record their work around the image of a flower, but I also really wanted to use the real thing. Then it all clicked into place. What if I combined the ideas? What if I made a worksheet out of a real flower?

This was brilliant: not only would I have the best of both worlds, but I would also be able to demonstrate my mastery of the school's newest and most cutting edge technology: the laminator.

It's difficult to describe the excitement of the laminator to a generation of teachers who have never battled with a roll of sticky-back plastic. Basically, it was the most popular piece of equipment in the school and teachers would happily queue in order to produce their smooth and shiny resources.

My plan was to place a flower in the laminating pouch, then send it lovingly into the machine so that I'd get a nice pressed flower worksheet emerging from the other side.

I was fully prepared for the flower to be squashed. I knew that would happen. What happened next took me completely by surprise.

Apparently, if you squash a flower, liquid, which I believe could well be water, seeps out of the stem. This caught me off guard.

The second surprise was that water and electrically powered laminating machines are not a good mix.

As the machine started to smoke, I tried to remove the pouch, which by this point had melted around the roller due to the heat of the small electrical fire that had sprung up inside the machine.

It's difficult to walk away from an incident like this without being noticed and even harder when the annoyingly sensitive smoke detectors set off the school alarm.

I returned to my classroom a broken man and reverted back to my original plan. (I didn't mean for this to rhyme, but as I've written it, I've had to resist the urge to go back and rewrite the entire story as a poem. That first floor's got a lot to answer for.)

As I said earlier, I'm not a fan of the whole Ofsted grading system, so I won't waste your time telling you what grade I was given. Let's move on.

While this mishap temporarily derailed my attempts at first-floor thinking, it didn't put me off completely – after all, you can't keep a good guerrilla down. Fortunately, I didn't have to wait too long before having another crack at the flower business as, shortly after the laminator incident, I was moved to Year 6, where, as luck would have it, the big children needed to know about flowers too.

To begin with, I'd decided that being creative was a mistake, and I just needed to go for totally normal lessons. I thought that you were either a creative teacher or not a creative teacher. I've come across this with other teachers too, and it can sometimes be a deeply held belief: 'I can't do that kind of thing – I haven't got a creative bone in my body.' It's rubbish, of course, and I started to realise that, like most things, it's not black and white. Creativity, like a lot of our skills or attributes, presents itself on a spectrum. We're all creative; it's just that we're at different points on the scale. Along with this, I genuinely believe that it's not fixed, and regardless of where you sit on the scale, there's always the opportunity to edge a bit further up.

I really like the idea of growing creativity, being a little bit creative, then a little bit more creative, then a little bit more. I like it because it allows us all to develop our first-floor thinking, but in our own time, on our own terms and while managing the elements of risk along the way.

So ignoring the 'all or nothing' thinking, you can start to take some of the 'dull but important' learning I talked about earlier and develop creativity bit by bit.

Lesson 1

Creativity:))))))
Risk:))))))
(rating system out of 5, where
))))) is most creative/risky)

If we go back to the lesson I'd tried to deliver in Year 1, the outcome was about the parts of a flowering plant. It was pretty straightforward and revolved around about five basic bits of key language. With upper Key Stage 2 children, things get more complicated.

Decide the outcome

Along with the basic structures, there's also some learning to do about the parts that are inside the flower. As an objective, we need to be thinking about the learning, and also the outcome. We want the children to learn about the parts of a flower, because if they do that, they'll be able to describe its structure as the outcome. To help with this (and to avoid a ridiculously long learning objective) we can borrow from one of the scripts we used earlier: 'Today we're going to be describing the structure of a plant, and to help us, *we are learning to identify and name the parts of a flower.*'

If we think back to Bloom's wheel, *'describe'*, *'identify'* and *'name'* are all verbs that fall within the first two sections of the wheel – Remembering and Understanding – which feels like a good start for any new piece of learning.

Identify the steps

As there's quite a bit of new learning for the children to get to grips with, it has to be broken down into manageable chunks. A bit like the Year 1 lesson, we'll definitely need modelling in there, and then plenty of opportunity for them to practise. To keep interest and interaction high, we're going to use real flowers, probably one between two or three children. One option would be to model the dissection of the flower, taking it apart bit by bit, then ask the children to do the same. It's clear, straightforward and the children would see exactly what they had to do. This might be too much information, though, and the children would find it difficult to remember and process it all. Instead, we could model the first part, maybe removing the petals, then send them off to do the same. This would bring with it the added advantage of slowing everything down (there's only one thing to do rather than a list to race through), we can now get the children to focus really carefully on the petals, noticing how many there are, their colour, structure and all the details that might have been lost in the rush.

When the petals are removed, the children would come back, we'd discuss what they'd noticed, I'd model the next section, and they're off again.

Download ...

Process ...

Apply ...

Repeat.

Review the language

Now that 'leaf', 'stem' and 'petal' will no longer cut it, it's time to fall back on the busy teacher's best friend, Wikipedia. As with lots of Internet-based resources, you have to be careful (there are occasional blips in the vast amount of information offered up). My favourite error occurred on the page dedicated to the philosopher Plato, who was described as being an 'ancient hawaiian weather man and surfer'. With plants, however, we should be on pretty safe ground, and I think its advantages outweigh its problems, besides, having used it as a starting point you could always check things out using a more reliable source such as the Encyclopaedia Britannica. One of the best things about doing a bit of research is that you end up finding out more than you need. Just because the curriculum states where the learning starts and stops, doesn't mean I can't take the children further if they're capable.

So with that in mind, here goes:

Key language	Definition	Bonus language
Stamen	Male part – makes pollen	Filament and anther
Carpel	Female part (stigma, style and ovary)	
Stigma	Traps the pollen	
Style	Connects stigma to ovary	
Ovary	Protects and stores ovule	Ovule

With the learning clear, steps identified and language distilled down to the bare essentials (card + trusty black marker + adhesive tack!), we're ready to crank up our first floor and apply some creative thinking.

Engage the heart

Just by thinking carefully about its structure (and because the children get to handle a real flower), we're already well on the way to an engaging lesson. The option we went for followed the Download, Process, Apply and Repeat model, so there's plenty to keep children involved and on task. To take things a step further we can look at selecting and using some of our quick-fire engagement techniques to add a touch of fun to the process.

Use of voice

Wherever there are words to be learned, there's shouting/whispering/singing or barking (sergeant-major style – not dog) to be done. We could also use one of our accents to lift the boredom of getting the children to repeat the language, or maybe have them follow up the keywords with their best 'evil scientist' laugh.

Mwahahahahahahahahah!

As well as singing the odd keyword, why not shoehorn all the key language into a song?

This little number goes to the tune of 'When the saints go marching in'.

Now we can name,

The flower parts,

Now we can name the flower parts …

STAMEN, STIGMA, STYLE and OVARY,

Now we can name the flower parts!

We even know,

Which bit is which,

We even know which bit is which …

The STAMEN is the male part,

And the CARPEL is the girl!

Admittedly, it's not the greatest song in the world, and it lacks any kind of rhyme, but on the upside it only took me five minutes to rattle off. As it won't fit on one of my little bits of card, this goes onto my big roll of lining paper (try any wallpaper/DIY shop – buy one big roll and it'll last all year). Just like the keyword cards, it's written in marker pen and stuck up on the wall, ready to return to at a moment's notice. Children love a bit of singing, and it's amazing how quickly they'll remember the lyrics. When you've written one, you'll find it hard to stop, and before long you'll have created songs and raps for all sorts of different kinds of learning.

Along with the singing, we could add movement by sticking our strips of keyword cards or song lyrics off to one side so we're mixing up our position in the classroom. After the children have repeated the key language enough times, we could throw in a bit of competition by covering the words up and challenging our pupils to recall them from memory. If we were feeling particularly brave, we could up the ante with the singing by getting them to do the song as a round!

Taking it up a notch, we could utilise some props. If you're not already wearing your 'mad scientist' eyebrows, then now is the time. Whip them out and stick them on or, better still, stick them on a child. As it's science, you can also get out your lab coat, because there's no point doing science if you don't look the part.

This could extend to Check the learning, which we'll be doing throughout the lesson. We might decide that we'll make use of the scientific research team and have our group of experts clipboarded up and ready to go with key questions for their peers. They could also be charged with collecting data from the whole class: Are all the flowers exactly the same? Do they have the same number of petals? What about the number of stamen? How could you present this data to the rest of the class?

Other means of checking learning present themselves through a combination of different levels of questioning:

Which part is this?

(Remembering – identify and name)

Have a look at our keyword cards – what job does it do?

(Process)

I wonder why it's that shape?

(Wondering)

Without going any further, you've already got the makings of a pretty good lesson. The learning's clear, and you've got a selection of quick-fire incidental bits of fun to choose from that can be dotted throughout the session to keep your young scientists engaged.

Before moving on, we'll cover the last aspect of our creative thinking process.

Troubleshoot and tweak

The more practical a lesson, the more potential it has for going wrong. We've already done a fair bit of troubleshooting as we've moved through the other sections. We decided to slow the learning down by breaking up the dissection bit, and we've made sure there'll be no babbling, thanks to the key language cards. Another example of the tweaking process takes us back to the idea of putting ourselves in the children's shoes. Imagine being a child about to go back for the first stage of the dissection. They're sharing a flower because their teacher was too tight to buy a bigger bunch. They can't wait to get stuck in and are determined to be the first to get their hands on the unfortunate tulip. Unfortunately, their partner feels exactly the same way. Now multiply that by a couple of times to take into account the other strong-willed children who, by some terrible coincidence, have ended up paired together. Within seconds we've got a battle on our hands.

Fortunately, though, because it occurred to us beforehand, we can avoid all this unpleasantness with a simple Partner A and Partner B system. Everyone knows where they stand, and nobody fights to be first.

Seemingly insignificant micro-decisions like these can have a significant impact on the success of a lesson, and the more time we spend tweaking at this stage, the better our lessons will be.

Lesson 2

OK, we've done the straightforward lesson. We added quick-fire engagement, and the lesson that came out of the other end was one that most of us would be happy with. But what if we wanted to go further? What if we really started to push your first-floor thinking? What if you flick the connections switch?

If you already view yourself as a creative thinker, then you've probably been cursed with a faulty switch. I say 'cursed', because it's this element of creative thinking that frequently becomes un-turn-off-able.

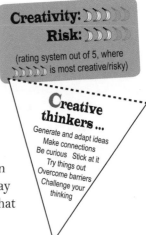

Creativity: ⟫⟫⟫
Risk: ⟫⟫⟫
(rating system out of 5, where ⟫⟫⟫⟫⟫ is most creative/risky)

Creative thinkers ...
Generate and adapt ideas
Make connections
Be curious   Stick at it
Try things out
Overcome barriers
Challenge your thinking

Traditionally in schools, when we start thinking about a creative curriculum (a proper creative curricular, not the kind that just happens on a Friday afternoon), we start by making connections between different areas of learning, and we call these connections cross-curricular links. The aim of this is to give purpose to learning and to help children see the connections between different areas of the curriculum. Planning formats often have a special box for cross-curricular links, and when putting together topics we might decide to link

English with history, and maybe throw in a bit of design technology (DT) too. This has to stop.

It's not the connections that I want to stop; more the way in which we think about them, as this thinking is causing a number of problems:

Problem 1: Thinking inside the box

Cross-curricular links are exactly what they say on the tin. They're meant to get us thinking creatively, but all we're encouraged to do is make connections between a fixed set of subjects. Sometimes, rather than appear un-creative because we couldn't find a cross-curricular link for our lesson, we'll fill the box in anyway with something tenuous, and before we know it, we've linked fractions to expressive dance. It's a good thing to make connections between different areas of the curriculum *when it works*, but why just limit ourselves to subjects when the world is our oyster?

Solution

To help us get the most out of our ability to make connections, we've got to widen and broaden the opportunities for finding a purpose for learning. To do this, we need to forget about links and instead think about context.

If we think about even the most straightforward, ordinary version of the flower lesson, we've got the opportunity to make a cross-curricular link with English. The children have done something (investigation) so now we can make a link with

'GET RID OF THE BOX!'

English and get them to write it up (report). A link's been made, and it's given the writing purpose, but that doesn't make it creative, and just because *we* think this link will add value and purpose, it doesn't mean the children will agree.

Thinking about context gets rid of the box, frees us up to use absolutely anything to create purpose for our learning, and allows us the kind of thinking that makes the curriculum seem a much bigger and far more interesting place.

Problem 2: Blurry learning

Along with limiting our thinking, working with cross-curricular links can also get incredibly blurry. If I link English and history, for example, what am I learning? Am I developing my English skills, or building historical knowledge? Remember, I've already talked about the idea of multiple learning objectives: it must be one or the other.

Solution: Keep the gods happy

If we're using cross-curricular links, when we've made the connections, there's a temptation to think that the hard work is done. In reality, it's only the start.

Imagine a scenario where we're doing the good old Tudors in history (for the twenty-fifth consecutive year). We make a cross-curricular link to English and decide to do a bit of persuasive writing (first-person persuasive letters from Henry VIII to yet another unfortunate young woman to convince her to marry him).

We're in our English lesson and we want the children to use persuasive language features, but because we've made the link with history, we're also talking about the kinds of things Henry might say based on historical knowledge. We're probably pretty pleased with the link we've made, but then the focus of the lesson starts to get a bit blurry. We set out with persuasive language firmly in mind, but we're side-tracked by a question from a child about Henry VIII. The question comes because they haven't got enough historical knowledge about Henry VIII and they need gaps to be filled. What do we do? Fill the gaps by launching into a bit of history while taking the risk that, as a result, their understanding of persuasive language will suffer? Alternatively, we could ignore it and plough on with the persuasive language, leading to decent English work but no historical accuracy?

There's no positive outcome here, and we end up with our head in our hands at playtime trying to work out what went wrong. In any given lesson where there's direct teaching going on, whether we've used cross-curricular links or not, we should always be able to say exactly what the learning is.

To sort this mess out, we need to get back to our use of the word 'context', because, along with providing us with great opportunities, it also makes these kinds of connections much clearer.

Cross-curricular link

English + history

Becomes:

LEARNING | CONTEXT

English | history

We're *learning* about persuasive language, and the *context* is history. Simple. And while this might seem like we're just saying the same thing in different words, the shift in thinking is important. Now that the learning is clear, we're much less likely to let anything get in the way of it. In fact, we're likely to make sure that nothing gets in the way. This forces us into thinking much more carefully about sequence.

If we're going to use a historical context, what do we need to do for it to work? What will the children need to know (and have at their fingertips) so that the learning in the lesson remains focused on English? If we're thinking in these terms, we'd be daft to even contemplate the English lesson unless it was following a sequence of several history lessons where the children had built up their historical knowledge with exactly this outcome in mind.

If we're starting history in week one, then there's no point in planning the persuasive writing unit until at least week three or four. If we get the sequence right, by the time we hit the writing unit, the children will have all the knowledge they need to apply their persuasive writing skills within the historical context. We'll have a nice clean lesson, the children will be successful, and the gods of English and history (or, at the very least, the subject leaders) will be satisfied with the outcome.

It feels like a lot to consider, just so we can have a bit of fun with the connections we make, but with this thinking firmly in mind, we can now start to explore just how far context can take us.

Recently, I met a Year 5 teacher who was in the second term of her NQT year and she told me a story about a night out she'd had with her friends just before Christmas.

The autumn term is always a bit of a killer, and if you're new to teaching, the main aim is to just get through it. This young teacher described being virtually on her knees. She'd made it through, but was utterly exhausted.

To celebrate making it, she'd planned a night out with her friends who were non-teaching (normal) people. In the first place they went to, her friends headed to sort out the drinks, while she slumped against the bar. As the group excitedly ordered cocktails, her attention was taken by the barman as he poured out, then mixed, the different quantities for the drinks. In that moment, like some terrible intrusive thought, all she could think was, 'I could use that idea when we do ratio and proportion'.

She didn't deliberately think it. She didn't want to think it. And in that single moment, it hit her that her life as she knew it was over.

Normal people leave work for the day, and have non-work related thoughts (I've been told this by friends). For us though, thanks to the faulty switch, we can't stop the random connections that pop up from completely unexpected places informing us that whatever we've just seen would be the perfect way to teach a particularly obscure bit of the curriculum. They can come from anywhere: out and about in town, in the middle of the woods, in the bath or, frequently, when I'm watching the telly.

Many TV programmes over the years have sparked some connection in my brain and ended up being used as a context for spicing up some dull but important learning. Some of my favourites are from pretty terrible shows, but nonetheless they made for exactly the kind of memorable lessons we're after.

Big Brother

A couple of years ago we had chickens in school. They were rescue chickens from a battery farm, and we'd agreed to give them a new home and some love and attention. When they arrived, they were a bit bald and sickly looking, and so one of our animal-loving teaching assistants decided to knit them some cardis to keep them warm at night. While this didn't go exactly to plan,[4] having the chickens living in a quad next to my classroom was an opportunity I wasn't going to miss.

At the time, *Big Brother* was in full swing, and while I wasn't really watching it (honest), I knew it was creating a bit of a buzz with the children. It occurred to me that the chicken pen, where we were keeping the newest members of our school community, reminded me of the cooped-up conditions that the housemates were experiencing in the Big Brother house.

As a result, I decided that we should use our chickens as the guinea pigs (!?) in our very own social experiment. I decided to turn the chicken pen into a Big Brother house for the brand new TV show, *Big Brother's Little Chicken*. My main reason for this was an upcoming unit in English on diary writing, and in the TV show, they have a special diary room where the housemates go to moan/complain/whine/talk about their day. If our chicken coop was the Big Brother house, what would our chickens have to say, and would the children be able to help them find their voice?

Without telling anyone, and much to the annoyance of the chief chicken looker-after-er (cardi-knitting TA), we transformed the chicken coop with fake cardboard

---

4   The chickens got their feet stuck in the hems, toppled over and then couldn't get back up. We found them the next morning lying on the floor coiled in masses of brightly coloured angora wool, bemused looks on their little beaky faces.

CCTV cameras, a diary room (an old cardboard box), and lots of signs and other *Big Brother*-themed accoutrements. When the scene was set, the children named the chickens and worked on building character profiles for them. To do this, they created an application form for each chicken that included details about personality, hobbies, likes and dislikes, etc. Following this, we worked on diary-writing skills by taking a day in the Big Brother's Little Chicken house, and turning it into something amazing (thanks to loads of sentence structure and language work). As the work came to an end, the children were filmed in a replica cardboard diary room dressed as chickens with inflated rubber gloves taped to their heads while they recounted the day's events via their first-person diary entries. Brilliant.

While this is arguably not a traditional approach to diaries, and first-person chicken writing does not explicitly feature in the curriculum, if we're not taking the opportunity to dress our children as farm animals, then they're definitely missing out.

Price Drop TV

Price Drop[5] was a TV shopping channel dedicated to selling some of the worst products ever invented. Now, while the products might have been pretty awful, the presenters were incredible. So incredible, that people all over the country couldn't get to the phone fast enough to bulk-buy as much rubbish as possible.

Having witnessed their incredible persuasive techniques, I saw how this could be used in school to give context to some persuasive writing.

After selecting a compilation of my favourite clips to show the children, they got to grips with the range of techniques that any self-respecting Price Drop presenters would need. What emerged were the common language structures and phraseology that could then be applied to sell pretty much anything to even the most disinterested of punters.

---

5   Sadly, Price Drop closed in 2014, but there are plenty of other channels out there that showcase best practice in effortlessly pedalling rubbish.

To test out the children's newly acquired skills, they needed a collection of junk that was almost completely useless. Again taking the chance to clear out my garage, I quickly filled a large box with rubbish.

Needless to say, the children rose to the challenge and came up with incredible ways to describe the junk and persuade potential customers to snap it up. In fact, they did so well that I let them keep their products and take them home as a special treat!

Big Cook, Little Cook

If you've got children under the age of five, you'll know this CBeebies classic only too well. Two chefs, Big Cook (who is regular adult size) and Little Cook (who is about the size of an Action Man) run a cafe. Storybook characters come in, and the chefs decide on a recipe to make. Big Cook then gets cracking while Little Cook swans off on a flying wooden spoon to investigate some aspect of the food production industry.

My two girls were big fans of the show when they were younger, and it didn't go unnoticed that I bore a strong resemblance to Big Cook. While telling my Year 6s about this at school, I bemoaned the fact that I've never been approached for television work, despite obviously having a face for it. Rather than sulking about it, though, I told them that I'd decided to create my own twist on *Big Cook, Little Cook* and begin my TV career with my very own show. (Remember the optimism I mentioned earlier? Despite the context being daft, embodying an 'anything is possible' attitude is an important part of your teacher persona.)

After explaining my idea, which involved branching out into the world of the celebrity travelling TV chef by wearing a cleverly adapted tool belt complete with all of the kitchen equipment a chef on the move would possibly need. (This involved another happy half hour spent in my garage – and several weeks of denial as my wife searched for the cheese grater.) I then began a unit on writing instructions that centred on creating recipes for my new celebrity cookbook. By the end of the work, not only had the children written some great recipes, but they were also generating pitches for their own TV shows which just goes to show, a little bit of optimism goes a long way.

I'll come back to the idea of creating different ways to build context a bit later on (page 131), but the reason I mentioned TV connections was because an idea I got from watching a TV programme led to the flower lesson.

At the time, I was into an American TV series called *CSI NY*, which revolved around a crime scene investigation unit in New York. Most of their work seemed relatively straightforward, and certainly nothing that someone with a teaching degree couldn't handle. Spurred on by the thought of using this idea with the children, I decided that I could have them learn all they needed to know about the parts of the flower via an autopsy.

This might seem grim, but I was confident that I could do it without upsetting and/or scarring anyone too badly. Obviously, if you're conducting an autopsy, there must have been a murder, and if there has been a murder, then there must be a crime scene.

When I have an initial thought about a context, it's often followed fairly rapidly by lots of other ideas to make it better, bigger or grander. This is the first floor really kicking in, and it's one of the joys of teaching for me.

It led to me thinking, If there's going to be a crime scene, we'd better tape it off. I wonder where I could get some tape? When the flowers are on the ground, maybe I could draw chalk outlines around their little bodies. On *CSI*, they always number the evidence with little cards. I could make some of those. And before long, I had prepared a realistic crime scene in a previously unassuming area of the school. So, with the crime scene set up, let's get on with the lesson.

Because we've already spent time focusing on learning in lesson 1, we can keep the lesson's carefully thought-out structure and enhance it with our creative context.

The lesson will begin with the introduction of the crime scene. How this happens can go one of two ways:

Option 1:

'OK, children, today we are going to be describing the structure of a plant, and to help us, we will learn to identify and name the parts of a flower. In a minute I'm going to take you through to a crime scene where we'll collect a flower before bringing it back to the classroom for the examination.'

This is a low-risk approach. It's low risk because to a large extent, the joy and excitement have been sucked out, thanks to the teacher playing things very straight. Just because the learning objective is our first port of call when we're thinking up the lesson, doesn't mean it has to be the first thing that's served up when we're in the classroom. If I had a class of particularly excitable children and I was worried about them going through the roof, then I may well decide to play things down a bit. However, if you've gone to the trouble of creating the crime scene, you're probably brave enough to risk whipping the class up into a (manageable) frenzy with a bit of acting. In which case, hold off on sharing the outcome, and kick off with the fun.

Option 2:

Pre-lesson preparation: Talk to a teaching assistant or other adult beforehand and get them to enter the classroom with an urgent message (the kind that can't be ignored!):

'Mrs TA, what on earth's the matter? Why are you rushing about like that?' (*Instant interest from children – something's afoot*)

(*TA approaches front*)

'What's that, Mrs TA? Something's happened?'

'I'm really sorry, children, but I need to listen to this, I don't know what's going on.'

TA and teacher move to one side and whisper (*children desperately try to overhear what they're saying*).

'Now children, you won't believe this, but something terrible has happened.'

Pause.

'Something truly terrible.'

Pause.

'Something truly, truly terrible.' (*Anticipation building …*)

Pause.

'Something truly, truly, truly terrible.' (*Almost too much for them to take …*)

Pause.

Pause.

Pause.

'There's been a crime.'

'A terrible crime.'

'A terrible, terrible crime ...' (*you get the idea*)

'I'm going to show you the victim ...'

'Do you think you can handle it without being upset?'

'Are you sure?'

'Are you really sure?'

'Really?' (*I never get bored of this!*)

'OK, here they are ...' (*produce flower from mocked-up evidence bag*)

'Look at it! A poor flower, cut down in its prime ...'

'Now the thing is, children, there's not just one victim – there's a whole crime scene.'

'We need to go and investigate, but we've got to be professional about it, haven't we? We've got to go slowly, calmly, quietly, just like scientists. Show me that you're ready.'

And with our classroom/behaviour management scripts feeding into the context, we're ready for the big reveal. Thanks to the build-up, on seeing the crime scene, the children are likely to react in exactly the way we want – with laughter or, better still, feigned horror at what lies before them.

After allowing the buzz to settle, we can get on with doing our job – collecting the victims and heading back to the crime lab. (Incidentally, despite children never having heard their classroom being referred to as the crime lab, they seem to accept this completely and know instinctively where to go!)

Back in the lab, the young scientists gather round the front to witness their teacher (the head examiner) don his white coat (two sizes too small) and start to model the autopsy, carefully removing and naming all the parts of the flower that we're interested in. We'd then follow the structure we planned in lesson 1 by slowing things down so that excitement doesn't overtake the learning, and each part of the flower gets the attention that it deserves.

As the lesson unfolds, there might be further elements from lesson 1 that get a new twist, thanks to our CSI context. The Partner A, Partner B bit, for example, could be framed with roles rather than letters. The children will swap roles throughout to avoid scrapping over the flower, but this time we could give them badges labelled 'Chief examiner' and 'Head of operations'. This immediately adds value to the experience, and gives us the chance to spell out our expectations of each of the roles. We could also up the ante when having the children feed back their findings. Rather than just stopping and letting them say whatever they've noticed, we can add additional layers of importance, with the children taking it in turns to don the lab coat and tell the class their findings via a departmental meeting!

If we still wanted to 'link' our science to English, then we could, but thanks to some creative first-floor thinking, we've opened up some far more interesting possibilities.

Perhaps the children could present their learning in a variety of ways – have a look at these ideas:

- Autopsy report (frequently overlooked as a genre in writing!)
- Newspaper report (covering the crime, but also clearly identifying the flower parts, so that readers understood the anatomy of the victim!)
- *Perennial Problems* (a new TV show that's a cross between *Crimewatch* and *Gardeners' World*?)

Thanks to the children's heightened motivation, we'll sail into our English work with purpose and a genuine need to learn. In addition to this, because there's something bigger going on here in terms of the crime scene, we're not tied to the straightforward report we'd be doing had we merely made the cross-curricular link.

Here are some ideas for CSI badges that you can use.

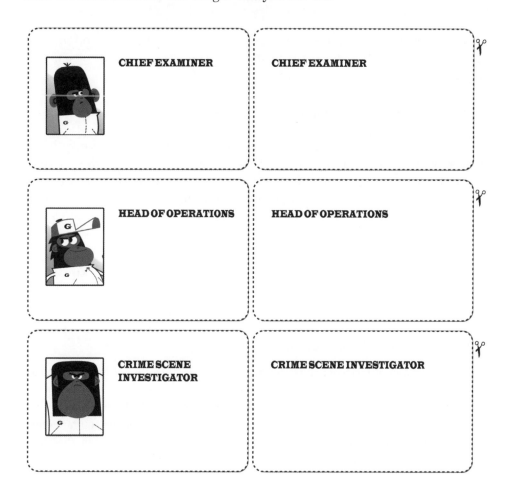

Risk

There's no doubt that this lesson presents more risk than lesson 1, and most of our apprehension will revolve around the two main ways in which the children might respond.

Problem 1: Over-excitement, leading to chaos

In terms of them getting over-excited and too carried away to work with any purpose, we've deliberately structured the lesson to make sure we strike the right balance between engagement and focus on learning. Our behaviour management scripts take into account the context of the lesson, but if these fail, we can always walk to our 'summat's up' spot to deliver the kind of straight-faced reminder that will get things back on track.

If you're a teacher who never works in this way, then it will come as a bit of a shock to the children, and you're likely to be in trouble. (In this case, it's better to revert to lesson 1: start small and build.) Alternatively, if you're producing lessons like this, day in, day out, you're also in trouble, because (a) you'll burn out before Christmas, and (b) the children will be so used to it that they won't bat an eyelid, and the lesson's impact is lost.

The ideal for a creative teacher is to find a happy balance by using high-impact lessons like this once in a while. It may be once every two or three weeks for the brave, or once every half term if you're testing the waters. In between times, we should be sprinkling bits of low-key playfulness and quick-fire engagement throughout our teaching, which means that we're highly likely to get the right response when we need it (more on this in Chapter 13).

Problem 2: They think that it/you are childish/stupid/idiotic

What if they don't go with us? What if they think it's stupid? What if they burst our bubble and refuse to play along?

It's an interesting one, this. The lesson described above is intended for older children (upper Key Stage 2). I know for a fact that they don't believe the crime scene is real, and my introduction of it relies on humour and is deliberately tongue-in-cheek. As a result I've found that children happily play along because they know they'll have a better time than if they sit and refuse.

If I had to go back to Year 1, however, and use a similar context, I would definitely use a different approach.

The crime scene scenario is ultimately based on a lie. I lied to the children about a crime happening. I don't feel bad about this, because the older ones all knew it was a lie. That was fine. The problem with younger children, however, is that they tend to believe everything we say.

I have to hold my hands up and say that I was a prolific liar while in Year 1. I would make up all sorts of things to get the children engaged in their learning, but then something happened that stopped me in my tracks.

When my younger daughter Imogen was in Key Stage 1, one of her teachers, a highly skilled and brilliant professional, decided to use a crime scene context to get the children engaged in a piece of writing. Using the text *Burglar Bill* by Janet and Allan Ahlberg as a theme, she set up the classroom to reflect the scene of a crime. Tables were overturned, chairs tipped over and other general mess was created. There was even a trail of talcum powder footprints leading mysteriously out of the door. As you can imagine, there was a real buzz when the children arrived at school, and before long they were asking questions and making suggestions about what might have happened. This led into their English work and at the end of the unit they produced a piece of writing that was in all likelihood brilliant. As the work was unfolding, Imogen was full of it and we got various updates on how their investigations were progressing. At the end of it, she did her writing and the class then moved on to something else. About a week and a half after the unit ended, I was summoned to her bedroom after lights out for what I presumed was just one more question that absolutely had to be answered before she went to sleep. It turned out I was right. Imogen had a question about the people who had 'burgled' the classroom. She wanted to know if they were still in school, and if they were, what if they took her?

This was over a week later, but in some corner of her mind, there was this seed of anxiety. If they were still in school, what if they came back?

It made me think about the lies I'd happily told my Year 1s, and older children for that matter, and it made me wonder whether I'd done something similar to them. This came as a bit of a blow, because all of a sudden I felt my days as a creative teacher were numbered. The chance that even one child in my class could leave a lesson feeling worried or anxious meant that it just wasn't worth the risk. But if I couldn't lie to children any more, then how could I create those brilliant made-up scenarios that would turn dull stuff into memorable lessons?

Fortunately, a solution presented itself pretty quickly, thanks to an incredible book I was reading about an incredible woman (*Dorothy Heathcote: Drama as a Learning Medium* by Betty Jane Wagner). Dorothy Heathcote was an educationalist who worked at the Newcastle Institute of Education between the 1960s and the 1980s. She was a drama teacher who used the method of teaching in role to access other areas of the curriculum. In keeping with the dishonesty I'd been up to, lots of her work began with a 'big lie', but the difference between her lies and mine were that, in her work, the children were in on the deception from the start.

To begin with, this seemed like a bit of a cop-out. If we tell them that it was us who burgled the classroom, set up the crime scene, planted the dinosaur egg or wrote the letter from the king, then surely the magic is gone? Why bother in the first place if we're going to reveal all from the start?

What I failed to take into account, though, is the single biggest thing that our youngest learners (and older ones, when given the chance) have got going for them: their imaginations. What if, instead of pretending things were real, we took a leaf out of Dorothy's book and invited them into a story instead?

Let's go back to the flower and the lie I told at the start. While we'll get away with it in Year 6, we can't tell five-year-olds that there's a murderer loose in school. What we need is a different script; a script that allows us to use the crime scene, but makes it clear to the children from the start that this is all just a story and not in any way real. After a bit of digging, I came across a really helpful blog by Tim Taylor,[6] a teacher, trainer and advocate of Heathcote's work.

Taking the ideas that Tim suggested around introducing the story, our script would look something like this:

'I've been thinking about a story, and in the story, there's a crime. To start the story, we're going to go to the crime scene, but we're not going to go as ourselves, we're going to be crime scene investigators.'

6   See http://www.imaginative-inquiry.co.uk/2014/08/why-telling-the-truth-is-better-for-learning/.

Doing it this way, we'll still generate the buzz of excitement we had before, but with no sleepless nights for our children – or awkward complaints from parents.

In addition to this – and more importantly – we're also shifting the responsibility for creativity. When we're teaching creatively, it's us demonstrating and modelling our creative thinking to children. This is good because modelling works, but unless we can find opportunities for them to get in on the act too, we're wasting our time. Using the story allows us to involve the children as co-creators from the start.

If we ask, 'Before we go to the crime scene, what do you think we should take with us?' Before long, we'll be swamped with suggestions from children who are using their creative thinking to add to the 'story' and develop it further. If you were feeling really brave and you wanted to push their imaginations, you could have the children mime getting ready: 'Remember to put on your special suit. Have you got your gloves? Are you ready to pack your investigator's case?'

Now we're really on a roll, the children are up for it, and we can get on with the business of learning.

What this approach also does is handily get over the tricky Year 3/4 period of disbelieving. If you imagine pitching the crime scene (as a lie) to this age group, we'll have a number of them believe it quite happily, but then the more streetwise among them will know that it's made up and, because of their age, feel compelled to share this knowledge with everyone else to prove that the wool has not been pulled over their shrewd little eyes: 'You made it … You wrote it … You put it there … It's not real …' And before you can silence the little tinkers your parade is well and truly rained on.

If it's a story, then there's nothing to prove and even the most cynical of eight-year-olds won't be able to get in the way of the brilliant experience you've got planned.

Chapter 9

BREAKING THE RULES

Building creative context

Everything we've looked at so far constitutes the basic make-up of a guerrilla teacher. Ground-floor and first-floor thinking are our bread and butter and they make a huge difference to our children, but dressing up, false eyebrows and shouting random words will only take us so far. Traditionally, whenever guerrillas are really up against it, rather than retreat into their shells, they come out fighting. Adversity makes them braver and, if anything, even more willing to take risks. If we're to follow in their footsteps, then we need to develop a similar disregard for rules and a healthy intolerance of rubbish.

We'll start with the little phrase that dominates the primary national curriculum: 'Children should be taught to ...'. This is what we're told to do. It used to be about learning, but not any more – they sit, we teach, then we give them a test to check it all went in. There we have it. A narrow view of learning cobbled together by a narrow selection of publicly educated narrow-minded people.

So if we're going to ignore this, then what do we do instead?

When we first looked at our all-important first-floor creative teaching, we were motivated by the fact that, if we model stuff, there's a very good chance the children will learn it. We model creative thinking, and the children will learn creative thinking. For this to be effective, though, there has to be the opportunity for practice.

If we're constantly 'teaching' children, then – no matter how creatively we're doing it – they're not going to get the opportunities they need to develop their own creative thinking, and we'll be as guilty as the numbskulls who thought up the curriculum in the first place.

Here's a timely reminder about why we're here:

To be a member of an unofficial group of combatants using the element of surprise to harass a larger less mobile target.

I don't know about you, but I think we've found a target, and we're about to throw everything we've got at it by doing the exact opposite of what we're told.

Chapter 10

THE ROOFTOP TERRACE: CREATIVE LEARNING

Refusing to do something without having an alternative is just sulking. Fortunately, we've still got an entire floor of Guerrilla HQ dedicated to actively ensuring that our children get plenty of opportunities to develop and practise their creative thinking.

We've done the groundwork and we're modelling our own creativity, but now we're about to head upstairs and create the right conditions for our children to learn for themselves. Welcome to the GHQ rooftop terrace.

If you're feeling slightly nervous at this next step on the road to becoming a guerrilla teacher, then you're not alone. There was relative safety on the first floor because, although we were working creatively, we were still in control. Now, though, things are different.

Regardless of what you call it – child-led learning, creative learning, discovery learning – it can be a pretty frightening prospect for anyone who teaches from Year 2-ish up.

These fears are not unwarranted. We're under a lot of pressure; we've got tight timetables; and then there's the worry about chaos. *If I let them learn for themselves, what if they don't learn what I want? Worse, what if they don't learn anything at all?*

We need to get over this, and how we do this is more to do with how we view this approach than the actual approach itself. First of all, let's clear up the misconceptions. Child-led learning, or creative learning, does not mean leaving them to it. This doesn't happen anywhere (or it shouldn't), and if you're lucky enough to have spent any time at all in foundation stage classes, you might have spotted the reality behind this myth.

Imagine walking out onto an empty foundation stage playground and putting down a box of differently sized sticks collected from the local woods. If you retreat to the safety of the classroom and watch as the children are released, you're likely to see one of two things.

1. Children (particularly boys) using the sticks as weapons.

2. Children (frequently girls) using the sticks as a wand. (In my school there are several girls who also go for the weapons in an attempt to challenge engrained gender stereotypes – bless 'em.)

While there will be a fair bit of creativity in their scope of weaponry (swords, guns, spears, rocket-propelled grenades, etc.), they will nonetheless be used as a means of destruction. While this is obviously a generalisation, it is something I've tried, and children do fall into predictable patterns of behaviour and play. Unless, that is, we do something about it.

A box of sticks is one of the best (and cheapest) resources that you could possibly use in foundation stage. There are endless opportunities for creative play and creative thinking – but to get there, the children need our help.

Here's the thing. While it might look like our youngest learners are just left to it, nothing could be further from the truth. Sticks are turned into telescopes, fishing rods, tepees, dream catchers, caterpillars, stirrers for cauldrons, rockets, musical instruments, animals, fairies, snorkels, conductors' batons, broomsticks and a whole host of other stuff too – thanks to the interventions of their teachers.

Creative learning does not mean adult-free learning, and if our job in the first instance was to model creative thinking, then what we've got to do now is help facilitate it.

Control

Chaos is the feeling of being out of control. There isn't any place for chaos in a classroom – or, for that matter, anywhere else in education. Chaos is frightening for both the children and for teachers. Having said that, the word 'control' doesn't seem to sit right with creativity either, but the kind of control we're interested in is applied as a framework for learning rather than something that inhibits the process itself.

If we go back to the sticks, to get the most out of this amazing resource, we'll need to pose questions, prompt and support the children to extend their thinking. We might help them to see how the sticks could be used to solve a problem or rise to a challenge.

All of the above requires thought. We need a structure to hang it on. A structure like this:

A bit like the Guerrilla Guide to Creative Direct Teaching wheel we used earlier (see page 56), this is also about a thinking process, and – more importantly – managing the chaos.

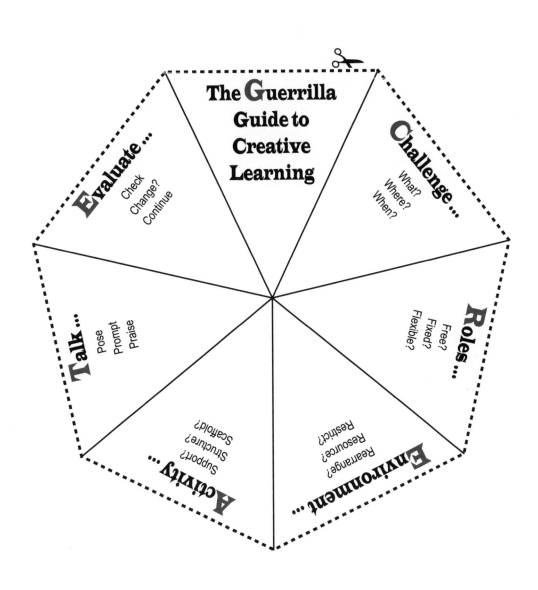

The Guerrilla
Guide to
Creative
Learning

Challenge...
What?
Where?
When?

Roles...
Free?
Fixed?
Flexible?

Environment...
Rearrange?
Resource?
Restrict?

Activity...
Support?
Structure?
Scaffold?

Talk...
Pose
Prompt
Praise

Evaluate...
Check
Change?
Continue

Chapter 11

CREATIVE THINKING WITH STICKS

There's nothing simpler than a stick, so it makes perfect sense (at least to me, anyway) to start by looking at how we can develop children's creative thinking with this handily accessible resource.

This time, instead of just dumping the sticks and leaving, we'll use the wheel to build as much potential for creative thinking as we can manage, while also avoiding the chaos. But before we get to the first section, we'll borrow a technique that we used earlier to slow things down and help the children to look more closely:

'I've got something here that I want to show you. Do you want to see? When we went on our walk through the woods we collected some sticks – do you remember? We've got all sorts of different sticks in this box – let's have a closer look.'

On taking the first stick out of the box, we can talk about its size, weight, texture or strength before passing it around for the children to hold. This is then followed by sticks of different shapes and sizes, and all the time, we're encouraging the children to describe what they can see and feel using their senses. (Although this is a pretty basic activity, helping the children notice the differences between the sticks will come in handy later.)

With the children slowed down and concentrating, and the sticks promoted to something now worth our attention, we can start to develop a purpose to use them.

Challenge: What? Where? When?

'When I was putting the sticks into the box this morning, I thought we might be able to use them to help with a story that we're going to make up together.'

'The story that I was thinking of happens on an island surrounded by the sea.'

'Let's make the outline of the island using some of our sticks.'

While this is directed by the adult, there's nothing wrong with a bit of a helping hand when it comes to viewing the sticks with a different purpose. What we're aiming for here is to encourage the children's imaginative eye – to get them to use simple things in imaginative ways.

'I wonder what the island would look like?'

This could be followed by the children adding more features to the island using the resources they had to hand, and when the island's established, then the story can begin:

'This morning, we're going to go to the island, but we're not going there as ourselves, we're going to go as a gang of pirates searching for some treasure.'

'Before we can search for the treasure, we need to get to the island.'

'I wonder how we could get across the sea?'

Using the idea of creating a big lie without any actual lying, we've arrived at the first challenge that the children will face. Now, before going any further, the entire story is not going to be played out solely using the sticks, but my choice of storyline is deliberate, and one that should allow us to get the most out of our zero-cost resource:

Section of story	Possible use of sticks
Beginning	Create an outline of the island
Travelling to the island	Boat Raft Bridge Airplane Snorkels …
On the island	Building shelters Making a fire Building traps Making a map Fishing …

Describing what happens next is tricky because we don't know exactly what the children will say. To remove a little bit of the uncertainty, dropping in some 'wondering' will allow us to prompt gently in the direction we're after, and it's fairly safe to assume that at least one of the ideas in the table above will crop up.

Roles: Free? Fixed? Flexible?

In thinking beforehand about how the story might unfold, and by subtly guiding the children towards considering different means of solving the problem, a number of potential roles will begin to emerge.

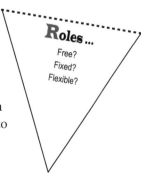

If we were to work on a single solution as a group, building a boat or raft, for example, then we could prompt the children to identify different tasks that would need to be completed:

'We'll need some people to be in charge of building the outside of the boat. 'I suppose that we'll also need to think about how it will move.'

'I wonder what we'll need to take with us ...?'

The roles would then be 'fixed' by organising the children into three groups, with each group working on a separate task.

If the children came up with several solutions to the 'crossing the sea' challenge, again we'd fix the roles to help us organise the different groups. One group might build a bridge, a second group a raft, and a third group might really go for it with a zip wire!

Environment: Rearrange? Resource? Restrict?

The way that we view the learning environment can also have a big impact on outcome. There's a strong temptation to make sure that we have everything to hand, to be resourced to the hilt, so that every conceivable piece of equipment is easily available.

Environment ...
Rearrange?
Resource?
Restrict?

We could have construction equipment at the ready, tubs full of modelling resources, sheets that would work for sails, ropes, balance beams, old tyres, art straws, modelling clay, glitter, but we don't need any of it to begin with, because we've got our box of sticks. Now, I'm not obsessed with sticks to the point where I'm not going to allow the children to use anything else. If the children decide they need some fabric for a sail, a rope or two to fish for sharks, or whatever else enters their imagination, then they can go off and find it when they're ready. What I'm not going to do is put everything on a plate and make life too easy. Over-resourcing can easily be a creativity killer, but thinking carefully about how we might restrict the children is a fantastic way of pushing them – and ourselves – to work increasingly creatively. After all, any fool can get to an island with unlimited resources; it takes a genius to do it with just a collection of sticks.

While we might restrict the raw materials, we'll need some resources in order to work with the sticks. String or twine for binding, secateurs for cutting and maybe a saw for the bigger sticks. (You hardly ever see young children using real hand tools – a massive shame.)

Because we know in advance that the children would be working with the sticks, we'd rearrange the space where they'll be working. Along with the box, I'd want to make sure that there were additional piles of sticks, branches and logs placed around the edges of the space for the children to access – but, beyond that, it would be pretty minimalist. The more room there is for the children to use their imagination and develop their thinking, the better.

Activity: Support? Structure? Scaffold?

We're already in a position where we're not only getting the most out of an incredibly simple resource, but we're also feeling a little bit safer about the experience, thanks to the structure.

Activity...
Support?
Structure?
Scaffold?

To further manage the now dwindling potential for chaos, we can also look at how we might support, structure or scaffold the learning.

In leading the children to think about some means of crossing the sea, we've given ourselves the opportunity to build a little bank of resources that might support or scaffold them on their journey – if needed. The 'if needed' bit is important. In an ideal world, the children would be buzzing about the challenge and bursting with ideas about how to cross the water, but what if they're not? What if they struggle to visualise anything that might solve the problem? For this eventuality, we need a backup plan.

In this example, it might be as simple as some pictures of different types of craft that could be used to cross water – a canoe (with paddle), a dinghy, a boat, a catamaran, a motor boat and water skier, a jet ski, a hovercraft or a raft.

We might build this collection further by sorting through the book box and selecting pirate-themed books with illustrations that might fire their imaginations.

If the children were struggling we could support them by showing the pictures and encouraging them to talk about what they could see. We could add further scaffolding by then making links to the resources at hand:

'If I use these two curved sticks, I can make the outline of the canoe. Could you make one too?'

'I wonder how big it would have to be for you to sit in it?'

And before you can finish the sentence, they're off.

Talk: Pose, prompt and praise

Dotted throughout the previous sections, there are little nuggets of questions and wonderings that we can ask to help feed the curiosity and imagination of our children so that they get the most out of our humble pile of sticks. The only real problem we've got now is shutting up for long enough for the children to have a chance to respond.

Talk...
Pose
Prompt
Praise

This might sound obvious, but teachers can be surprisingly adept at not just answering the children's questions, but also answering their own. It's a particular feature of upper Key Stage 2 teachers. We can't help ourselves – we know stuff and feel it's our professional duty to pass this on to our dear children.

It's the mindset of a teacher who has spent a lifetime on a diet of direct teaching and from experience; it's a tough habit to break. What I've learned, though, is that really great foundation stage teachers do something a bit different. Try asking a foundation stage teacher a question. They don't answer. You should definitely try this out. They're not being rude; they're just pre-programmed to keep what they know to themselves for the greater good of others. When you ask them something, instead of answering, they fire back another question.

Normal person: 'Can you tell me what time it is?'

Foundation stage teacher: 'What time do you think it is?'

Normal person: 'I'm not sure, that's why I asked.'

Foundation stage teacher: 'I wonder how we could find out?'

Normal person: 'We could find a clock?'

Foundation stage teacher: 'That's a wonderful idea. I wonder what the numbers mean?'

Normal person: 'They tell us the minutes and hours.'

Foundation stage teacher: 'That's really interesting. Can you read them? Let's count together.'

Together: 'One, two, three, four ...'

You'd be forgiven for thinking that this is extremely annoying, and there's no doubt that they must be very difficult to live with, but as a strategy for working with children, it's genius.

In the space of a short conversation, the teacher has assessed my prior understanding of how to tell the time, identified that I know something about the units of time, and is now taking the opportunity to reinforce my ability to count. All this because she refused to tell me that it was twenty-five past two, which in all likelihood is something she knew from the start.

If we feel that the children need a bit more support than can be given through questioning, then we can also use prompts to give some subtle suggestions:

'Would it help if ...?' (suggestion)

'What would happen if ...?' (suggestion)

'Have you thought about using/trying/finding ...?' (suggestion)

'If we started with this, what could you do next?' (modelling)

'Have you seen what Cameron has done? Could you use his idea to help?' (modelling)

As soon as an interesting response comes our way, we can use the third element of praise to let the children know that they're on to a winner. (Remember that we're not giving praise for them guessing what's in our heads, or for what we perceive to be a right answer, but for generating any form of interesting response that has the potential to lead to a purposeful outcome.)

'What a fantastic idea! Tell me a bit more.' (affirming and probing – sounds terrible, but you know what I mean!)

'That's brilliant thinking; I wonder what you might do next.' (affirming and speculating)

'That's an amazing idea, let's tell the other group.' (affirming and sharing)

With these three strategies added to our repertoire, we're well on the way to maximising the opportunities that come from withholding our expertise.

There's still a time and a place for giving a straight answer, but there's also a lot to be said for a bit of tongue-biting too.

Evaluate: Check. Change? Continue

Through our talk, we've already given ourselves plenty of opportunities to check what the children are thinking. In the vast majority of cases, thanks to the structure provided by the other sections, their thoughts will be purposeful and related to the task in hand. But what if they're not? What if our little monkeys appear to be doing something seemingly unrelated to our island challenge?

Evaluate ...
Check
Change?
Continue

If we notice children who appear to be off-task, or involved in something seemingly unproductive, we need to intervene.

This last section acts as a bit of a safety valve for exactly these moments – the times when we feel that things could be heading off the rails. Before we go any further, it's worth mentioning that the off-the-rails moment will be different for different people. For some, the feeling of chaos begins with the thought of children working in groups. For others, it might be the second that children start throwing furniture.

Clearly, the place to be is somewhere in the middle. If we had to go one way or the other, most of us would veer more towards the former. In doing this, though, we leave ourselves vulnerable to one of the biggest challenges in allowing children to work creatively – the temptation to wade in too soon. Thanks to the support, structure, scaffolding and prompting we looked at earlier, we'll have things at the ready that'll help to redirect the children if necessary, but if they're given too soon, or too late, we've got problems.

Intervening is something teachers are good at. We see something happening that doesn't match the idea that's in our heads, and then feel compelled to go over and sort it out. To get the most of the opportunities we've created, though, we need to stop – or at least delay it a bit.

Again, pinching from the foundation teacher's toolkit, we'll open with a question, because while it might look like nothing good will come of whatever it is the children are up to, they could well have a different, but no less valid, approach.

'Can you tell me a little bit about what you're doing?'

That was the easy bit. What comes next is more complicated, but thankfully it can be laid out in a user-friendly flow chart.

As you can see, the final outcome is relief, but how we get there is largely up to us. The ability to talk to children, take in their responses, and then make the kind of connections that would lead them back on track is a difficult thing to do in the heat of the moment. It relies on us having a spot-on (and broad) subject knowledge, so that potential connections are at our fingertips. If the connection doesn't come, there's nothing wrong with stopping, recapping on the task and starting again. After all, a dead end isn't a bad place to turn around.

Flow chart of what goes on in our heads and what comes out of our mouths!

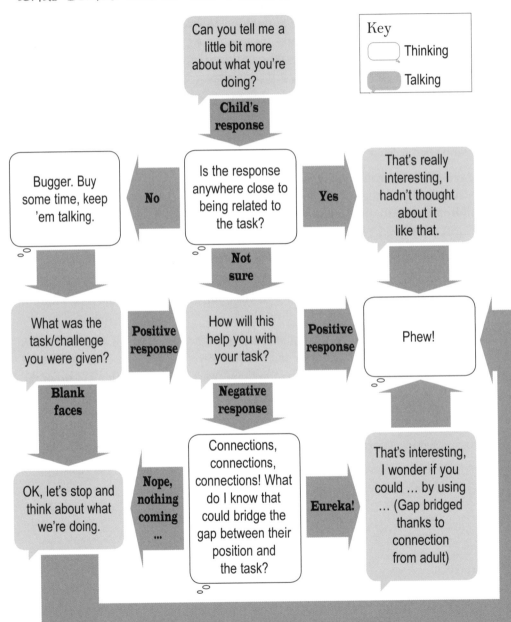

Chapter 12

CREATIVE THINKING WITH THINGS THAT AREN'T STICKS

Lesson 3

While I am undeniably a huge fan of sticks, there are plenty of other things out there that can also benefit from the same treatment. In lesson 2, the CSI flower lesson, I'd upped the creativity and risk to three. In this chapter, let's go further. Let's go all out, full-on guerrilla: 'I'm thinking about a story, and in the story, there's a crime.'

It starts in exactly the same way as before. We'd set up the crime scene and introduce the story to involve the children from the beginning. Previously, when we arrived back in the 'crime lab' with the flower victims, we modelled the autopsy for the children, using and repeating the key language. We taught the children about the parts of the flower. This time, we won't.

Instead of dishing up the knowledge, start with a question: 'Now that we're back in the crime lab, I wonder what we should do next?' You can almost guarantee that children will make lots of different suggestions around this, and what we're hoping for is that one of them will mention something related to finding out more about the victim. While we're definitely listening out for an idea that will help us with the learning we're interested in, we're not going to dismiss the children's suggestions just because they don't fit into our plans. We need a starting point, and there's nothing wrong with selecting the idea that will help us get to the learning we're after. A good way of structuring this would be to record the children's thoughts as you're going along on a big sheet of paper. When we've got everything, we can take a step back, look at the list, and employ a bit of thinking out loud:

'That's a brilliant list of ideas, we've got so much to do. We better decide where to start. I suppose that crime scene investigators would definitely want to know as much as they could about the victim. Let's do that first.'

With the starting point decided, we're ready to go, but sending the children off to just get on with it would lead us to exactly the kind of chaos that we're trying to avoid. Not only will the children be excited, but we also haven't given them even the slightest thing to go on. Fortunately, we can use the Guerrilla Guide to Creative Learning wheel to help.

This bit is pretty straightforward – the challenge is to find out as much as possible about the flower.

Challenge ...
What?
Where?
When?

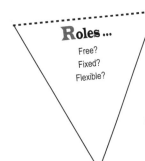

Roles ...
Free?
Fixed?
Flexible?

Just as in lesson 2, we'll make deliberate choices about the size of groups and who does what and when. They might be fixed groups to begin with, but you could easily introduce some flexibility by allowing the children to form groups that each focus on different elements of the flower. In the real world, there'd be several different forensic departments working on aspects of the investigation, so why not let the children do the same?

Given the way that we're co-creating the story, it would be easy to give the children the opportunity to rearrange their classroom to resemble a crime lab:

Environment...
Rearrange?
Resource?
Restrict?

'What could we do to turn our classroom into a crime lab?'

'How could we arrange the tables to help with our investigation?'

After making quick decisions about furniture, and the room set up and ready, we're almost good to go. In terms of resources, a bit like with the sticks, we're generally pre-programmed to give the children everything they could possibly need right from the outset. Reference books, iPad or tablets, sticky notes, key vocabulary cards, pencils, pens, sheets of paper, glue sticks – you name it, and we'll have it ready. This is even more obvious when we're being observed, and as the graph on page 153 clearly shows, the correlation between the stuff we put out and who's in the room is pretty striking.

There's a very good reason for these peaks. Self-preservation. Nobody wants the sack – we all want to do well and, in trying to do well, we cover every single eventuality and strip the lesson of any potential for even the slightest bit of fuss. If children need to stick stuff, there'll be glue sticks lined up on the table (brand new ones for Ofsted), and sharp pencils and new whiteboard pens will be added to pots (plus three spares of each for Ofsted). Carefully prepared sheets, books and anything else will be placed neatly in the middle until we're totally happy that everything is in place and nothing can go wrong.

Fortunately, we're not always under this kind of pressure, which means that, rather than aiming to make life easier for the children, we can play around with making it more difficult, or, at the very least, more realistic.

We're after desirable difficulties.[1] Just as with the sticks, we want children who are pushed to overcome barriers and make connections. Now, we're not expecting

---

1   Elizabeth L. Bjork and Robert A. Bjork. Making things hard on yourself, but in a good way: Creating desirable difficulties to enhance learning. In M.A. Gernsbacher, R.W. Pew, L.M. Hough and J.R. Pomerantz (eds), *Psychology and the Real World: Essays illustrating fundamental contributions to society* (New York: Worth Publishers, 2011), pp. 56–64.

them to cope with absolutely nothing, but restricting what they have from the start is an ideal way to introduce the level of difficulty we're interested in.

There's only one piece of equipment that I'd want the children to have at the beginning. More than anything else, I want them to look at the flower. I want them to look really closely. To signal this to the children, they'd have magnifying glasses at the ready – no paper, no pens, no books or anything else, just magnifying glasses.

Having looked, and noticed and discussed, there'll come a point where other resources will be needed. There's only so far that their existing knowledge and observations will take them, so there has to be the opportunity for them to somehow gain this new learning for themselves.

It's obvious, but even in our digital age, there has to be a place for real-life books. I've gone to incredible lengths in the past to help children access the information that they need. I've had piles of relevant reference books at the ready, with little coloured sticky notes sticking out to direct them to exactly the right place. At other times, I've photocopied the pages that will give them what they need so they don't waste time having to search.

When it's written down in black and white, this sounds ridiculous, but I bet it's something we've all done. We've grown up with the message that we need to get the children from A to B in the most straightforward, trouble-free way possible. We've been trained to remove the barriers to learning so that the path is clear, and while all this was happening, I forgot that books don't live on tables, they live on bookshelves or in a library. And because that's where they are in the real world, that's where they should be in the classroom.

To manage this without having all the children piling towards the bookcase and grabbing what they can, another little restriction comes into play.

As the children carry out their observations and talk to each other about what they can see, we could deliver a sticky note to each group with the following message.

Choose up to three books from the bookcase that will help you with your investigation.

In terms of preparation, we'd be idiots if we left the contents of the bookcase to chance. A 'less is more' approach doesn't really reduce the preparation we do. If

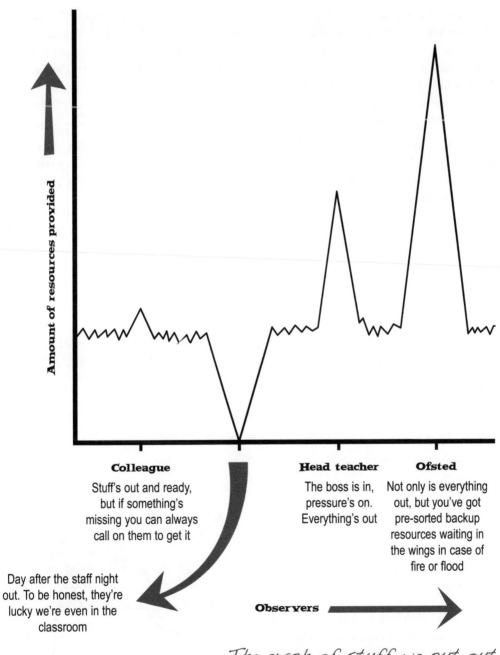

Amount of resources provided (vertical axis)

Colleague
Stuff's out and ready, but if something's missing you can always call on them to get it

Day after the staff night out. To be honest, they're lucky we're even in the classroom

Head teacher
The boss is in, pressure's on. Everything's out

Ofsted
Not only is everything out, but you've got pre-sorted backup resources waiting in the wings in case of fire or flood

Observers

The graph of stuff we put out vs people who are watching!

anything, it forces us to think even more carefully about what we're up to. If the children are going to go and select three books that they think will be helpful, I'll have made sure that there's a good selection (and number) for them to choose from. Equally, what'll happen if the books they choose turn out to be not so helpful? Do I want some kind of book swap system in place, or am I going to revel in their misfortune, in the knowledge that it might push them to search for another source of information?

This leads quite nicely on to 'other stuff' we might use. Beyond books, there might be iPads, tablets or laptops available for the children to access; again, 'available' is the keyword here. Technology is lovely, but we don't *have* to use it – and absolutely shouldn't use it, unless it enhances the learning.

Further practical resources could be made available via a CSI 'equipment room' (using a little card stand, a trusty black marker and a flat surface at the side of the classroom). I'd be tempted to throw in another level of challenge by collecting a range of useful resources and mixing them in with a selection that – at first glance – appear not to be so useful.

Useful items	Items that are not so useful (at first glance)
<ul><li>forceps</li><li>petri dishes</li><li>sticky notes</li><li>clear plastic bags (small)</li><li>scalpel (a plastic party knife – I'm not an idiot!)</li><li>paper towels (no lesson's complete without them)</li><li>rulers/tape measure</li></ul>	<ul><li>string</li><li>Lego</li><li>masking tape</li><li>modelling clay</li><li>banana</li></ul>

Again, the children would have to decide what to use and when. Items in the left-hand column are pretty obviously useful, but the right column offers things to either dismiss and ignore, or use creatively. Perhaps apart from the banana.

Now that we've sorted the environment, we can start to think about how we'll support, structure and scaffold the learning. Just making resources available doesn't remove the potential for chaos. What if the children can't access them? What if the information they find on the Internet isn't appropriate?

Activity...
Support?
Structure?
Scaffold?

Now this is definitely 'glass half empty' thinking, and maybe everything in the lesson will be fine, but as with the bookcase, why leave things to chance?

This is a bit of an odd section, really, because in an ideal world, we would do the preparation, but then never need to use it.

Problem	What you should have up your sleeves
Children can't access information in books (or get distracted by the cute pictures of piglets in the animal section)	Keyword cards These should include prompts about using the index and glossary to find relevant information that will help with their investigation. Can you use these clue words to help with your investigation? *stamen* *stigma* *style* *ovary* Use the index and glossary to help.

Problem	What you should have up your sleeves
Children are using the Internet but can't find age-appropriate information	**Child-friendly search engines** There are several handy search engines out there that throw up child-friendly sites with accessible language. Try these for size: ● KidRex ● KidzSearch ● Mymunka For older children, try the Simple English version of Wikipedia.[2] Go to the traditional version of Wikipedia (never far from the top of any search), then when you're on the page you're after, go to the 'Language' selection on the left, select 'Simple English', and the page magically transforms into something much more readable.
Children are using the Internet and can't find anything at all!	**QR codes** Creating QR codes is a handy way of ensuring that children access exactly the information they need, and they're incredibly easy to make (search on the Internet for a QR code generator, paste in your URL and print them out onto bits of card so they're ready for use). *Cont …*

---

2 I was blissfully unaware that this even existed until it was pointed out to me by Julian Wood, a thoroughly clever colleague and a very nice man.

Problem	What you should have up your sleeves
	Cont …
	If I'm honest, they're pretty much the digital equivalent of the sticky note sticking out of the relevant page in a book. Scan one, and you're transported straight to the stuff you need. In the unlikely event of completely fruitless research from the children, they're not a bad thing to have in reserve.
	Scan me and see for yourself!

Along with the potential sticking points above, there might be other problems that we anticipate and prepare for. This is exactly what the planning process is about but, like I said before, just because you've prepared it, doesn't mean you will have to – or should – use it.

Thanks to the challenge, the children are equipped with the desire to be successful, and they'll be desperate to find out as much as possible about the victim, the flower. Because of this, they're much less likely to be put off by barriers in their path, and as a result are likely to have an increased tolerance for struggle. Our job is to monitor the struggle so that it doesn't get to the point of frustration, and give support, structure or scaffolding just at the point that it's needed.

Given what we've already got in place, our use of Talk should come quite easily.

Talk …
Pose
Prompt
Praise

When posing questions, we can rely on the different levels I mentioned earlier. Download (Remembering), Processing,

Applying and the wonderings. We've also got our prompts that come in the form of suggestions and modelling.

To recap, here are some examples.

Question type	Poser or prompter
Remembering – demonstrating recall	What's that part of the flower called?
Processing – showing understanding	Can you explain in your own words the function of the stamen?
Applying – making sense and making links	Using what you've learned, tell me how flowers reproduce.
Wondering – hypothesising	I wonder why the leaf is that shape?
Suggesting – showing the way	Would it help if I gave you some clue words?
Modelling – leading the way	Let's start by looking at the petals, what could we do next?

Along with these questions, we've also got our use of praise to keep things nicely on track.

Praise	Effect
'I love the way you used that banana to demonstrate how plants are pollinated by insects.'	1. Child is buzzing – great! 2. Creativity is noticed and affirmed – great! 3. Everyone else is now clamouring for a banana – not so great!

Praise	Effect
'Everyone just stop for a minute and listen to what Ellie's just found out – this is incredible.'	1. Child is buzzing – brilliant! 2. An interesting line of enquiry is highlighted – also brilliant! (Especially if some children are in need of a bit of direction.)
'Let's hear from Fantastic group: can you tell everyone how you found out so much amazing information about the flower?'	1. Children are buzzing – fantastic! 2. The process is praised, not just the outcome – equally fantastic!

And if that's not enough to be going on with, you're probably talking too much, so keep it down and withhold your expertise!

Evaluate is the last piece of the puzzle, and it's the only section of the wheel that we can't really prepare for beforehand. Fortunately, thanks to the groundwork we've put in throughout the planning process, everything feeds into this point.

Evaluate ...
Check
Change?
Continue

Is the way that we've rearranged, resourced or restricted the environment supporting the children's learning? Yes? Continue. No? Change.

Is the support, structure and scaffolding of the activity doing its job? Yes? Continue. No? Change.

When this filters down to how the children are responding (and, more importantly, how we're responding to their responses!), we can use our trusty flow chart (see page 148) to help us intervene.

When rating this back at the start, I gave it a five out of five for creativity and a four out of five for risk. The creativity mark is up there because of what it allows the children to do. There's no teaching going on, but there is incredible learning, and the children are actively practising and developing their creative thinking skills.

From the start, the children are encouraged to generate ideas about what to focus on and how to work. Their curiosity is developed by looking closely and speculating; barriers are overcome by navigating restrictions and managing moments of challenge.

The openness of the lesson fuels the desire to stick at it, because who knows where the children might end up?

Creative thinkers ...
Generate and adapt ideas
Make connections
Be curious Stick at it
Try things out
Overcome barriers
Challenge your thinking

When applying the first floor of Guerrilla HQ to build lessons 1 and 2, there was a ceiling. When we decide the outcome of a lesson, we have a very clear idea about what the children will know or understand by the end of the lesson. In the first two lesson examples, I wanted them to know the parts of the flower and understand their function. If they can do this at the end of the lesson, it's been a success. There's a place for this, and it's sometimes the best option, but it doesn't take a genius to see the potential that lies in lesson 3. There's no ceiling on the Guerrilla HQ rooftop terrace (not even a canopy), and there's no ceiling on this learning. In my guerrilla brain, I know the things I'd *like* the children to discover, and I'll use the wheel to guide them in the right direction, but I'm equally open to them discovering things beyond the statements that are in the curriculum.

When working with a group of Year 5 children in this lesson, they had, thanks to using a range of resources, discovered the names and function of the parts of the flower. As they were looking for further avenues to explore, one girl called me over and asked about a word that she was struggling to read. The word was photosynthesis. After reading it for her, she seemed quite happy and continued to read the Simple English Wikipedia information on her laptop. A few minutes later, she called me over again to tell me what she'd found. After looking at the definition and talking to her friend, she'd come up with her own explanation of the process, that made sense to them both: 'I think that the leaf on a plant is a bit like a solar panel because it collects the sunlight and uses it to make energy. That's what photosynthesis is, isn't it? It's what the plant does with the sunlight to make its food.' This wasn't what was on the laptop screen; this was an idea that had come from piecing together bits of knowledge into one, simple, beautiful statement.

After the lesson I checked the curriculum, and it's nowhere to be seen in Year 5. It's not in Year 6 either. It's only when you get to Year 7 that it crops up and, had that ceiling been in place, we never would have got there.

Children can (and definitely should) be taught, but they should also be given the chance to explore for themselves, because when they do, they frequently learn a lot more.

PART III
Ongoing Strategy

Chapter 13

GUERRILLA STRATEGY

Before going any further, we should probably talk strategy. We've got a pretty impressive arsenal now, but we need to think about how best to use it.

We've got our ground-floor teacher persona, our first-floor creative teaching, and then the roof terrace dedicated to creative learning. What we're after now is the perfect blend that will help us to achieve our goals, while at the same time making sure that we're not so gung-ho that we render ourselves unfit for active service.

Every minute of every day

All those elements of our teacher persona are the bits we live and breathe. Interest and importance, happiness and optimism, curiosity, awe and wonder, playfulness, fallibility and not sucking your belly in are day-in, day-out, minute-by-minute characteristics. They're easy to cultivate, and as long as we check once in a while that everything's still ticking over nicely, these guerrilla traits will become automatic.

Lesson by lesson

When we looked at the first floor of GHQ and started to build our creative teaching in lesson 1, we looked at quick-fire engagement. There's a place for a Geordie accent in almost[1] every lesson, in my opinion, but beyond the accents there is a whole host of other stuff that we can add, lesson by lesson, without ever needing to plan for it. Whether it's reaching for a wand instead of pointing with a pen, belting out keywords at the top of our voices, throwing in some

---

1   The 'almost' is important. I've already addressed the dangers of yelling out keywords in sex education, and there'll be other areas of learning that you should treat with sensitivity rather than glitter. You have been warned!

competition with a two-minute challenge or whipping out our inflatables, there's a bit of incidental fun that can add sparkle to virtually any lesson we've planned.

One in fifty

Lessons 2 and 3 were about using context in standalone lessons. There's no doubt that, thanks to the crime scene scenario, these were high-impact lessons. We wanted our children to be buzzing about them and desperate to tell their parents what they'd been up to the minute they got home from school. If we follow this up with another bobby-dazzler full-on lesson the following day, then again on Thursday, however, it won't take long before the novelty wears off and our full-pelt creative teaching and learning becomes an expected daily diet. About ten years ago, when I got my first interactive whiteboard I had a class full of children who were blown away by the technology and the fact that I could write and move digital images around using some kind of magic pen. Their wonderment lasted just under forty-eight hours, after which they got bored with it and it was just wallpaper. If this happens with our lessons, then we're well and truly up the creek. Fortunately, the solution is simple, and also music to the ears of overworked teachers: Don't do it that often.

One in fifty lessons sounds pretty infrequent, but most of us will be teaching between twenty and twenty-five lessons a week, give or take, which means that a realistic aim might be to go all-out once every two weeks. Depending on your energy, the time of year or how creative you're feeling, you might be up for more, in which case you could go to one in twenty, or once a week. Having them spread out like this means that you get to enjoy the impact of them long after the lesson has finished. Following a high-impact session, there'll be a surge in excitement, motivation and engagement that'll carry the class through other, more straightforward, lessons on a wave of new-found enthusiasm for learning. This ripple effect shouldn't be underestimated and, when teamed up with the anticipation that comes from the children never quite knowing when something really great is going to happen, then we've created the perfect climate for learning.

Another factor linked to frequency will be your readiness to take risks and do things differently. How up for it are you? Are you prepared to go guerrilla and try stuff in the knowledge that, even with all your careful thought and planning, there's still a chance that things could go wrong? If you're giving something a go for the first time – whether it's a bit of creative teaching you've thought up or you're giving the children the chance to learn for themselves – you're much more likely to feel confident about it if you've battened down the hatches and made sure there's nobody watching. I think it's perfectly normal to want to do something risky out of the sight of others. If it goes wrong, it stays between you and the children – and I've always found them to be completely forgiving when it comes to trying out new things. With this in mind, I've included a handy door hanger at the end of this chapter to ensure that there are no interruptions that might curb your creativity. Stick it on your doorknob and away you go!

On the flip side, however (and on the flip side of the door hanger), is an invitation to come and have a look. As a guerrilla, if you've got great things going on in your classroom (and if you're feeling confident about them), then it's your duty to share the magic around. Think of it as recruiting others to our cause, whether it's the teacher from next door, or the boss. Let them in, show them what you're up to and spread the joy.

The more we try things out, the braver we'll get, and mixing things up and throwing in a bit of unpredictability is a key guerrilla tactic. Embrace your inner oddball. Keep things fresh, and keep your class guessing so they never know where the next creative bombshell is coming from.

Risky stuff happening. KEEP OUT!

Risky stuff happening. COME AND SEE!

Chapter 14

LARGE-SCALE MANOEUVRES

'Every time you do a project, you learn something new.'

Justin Timberlake

While high-impact lessons will take place once in a while, this doesn't mean we can't find other ways to build in opportunities for the children to develop their creative thinking. Striking the right balance can be made a bit easier by building topics, rather than just focusing on individual lessons, and it's here that the different elements of creative teaching and creative learning really start to come together.

Planning a project

One of the best ways to think about building a unit of work or a topic is to go down the project-based learning route. This can be a relatively straightforward approach, and one that lots of primary teachers (and Justin Timberlake) are pretty familiar with.

The difference between a rubbish project and a brilliant one is often down to a combination of the teacher's first-floor creative thinking and their willingness to venture up to the rooftop terrace – bringing together the best of both worlds. Introducing the unit in a monotone voice while clutching a pile of worksheets is not going to cut it, so we should spend our time thinking creatively about the connections we can make that will give some relevance and purpose to the learning and get the children engaged. Along with this, there's always the risk that, even with a creatively put together project, we could still default to the 'pupils should be taught' kind of thinking that will remove any opportunity for our children to take responsibility for their own learning by discovering or exploring things for themselves. To see how this might work, take a look at these little nuggets of knowledge from the current curriculum:[1]

Pupils should be taught to:

- recognise that they need light in order to see things, and that dark is the absence of light
- notice that light is reflected from surfaces
- recognise that light from the sun can be dangerous and that there are ways to protect their eyes
- recognise that shadows are formed when the light from a light source is blocked by a solid object
- find patterns in the way that the size of shadows change.[2]

Apart from the fact that you could teach at least two-fifths of these bullet points just by getting the children to shut their eyes really tightly, what we're really after is something a lot more memorable. What if we covered all of the objectives above (and probably a few more for good measure) by creating a project about photography?

This might seem a bit of a leap, but you only need to spend a few minutes searching for images on the Internet using words like 'light' and 'shadow' to be inundated with pictures that would make for an interesting starting point. To take things a step further, what if – instead of just researching or collecting photographs that showed the different effects of light we were after – the children composed and took the pictures for themselves?

Now we've made the connections, the next question to ask ourselves is why? It's all very well running around taking lots of nice pictures of shadows, but what's the point? What will happen to the photographs? I suppose they could be stuck in books, maybe displayed on the classroom wall, but that's all a bit ordinary.

---

1   The objectives listed here come from the Year 3 curriculum. Light then crops up again in Year 6 where children get to revisit and build up their learning with a few extra bits thrown in for good measure.
2   National Curriculum in England Key Stages 1 and 2 Framework Document (London: DFE, 2013).

GO BIG OR GO HOME!

What if we thought bigger, or created an outcome that had real purpose? Successful photographers exhibit their work in galleries, so why can't we?

With this in mind, we've got the nuts and bolts of our project sorted:

Central learning: Light

Context: Photography

Outcome: Create and open a gallery to showcase the class's work

Now we just need a way to start. Since we know where we're going, we're perfectly placed to work backwards to a starting point that makes sense. It would be a bit much to expect children to get the idea of opening a gallery if they've not experienced this for themselves, so it makes sense to plan a visit to a gallery so they can see one at first hand.

Any local gallery will do, and it doesn't really matter what's being exhibited as long as it's interesting and the children have a great day (check beforehand that it doesn't contain lots of eighteenth-century paintings of naked people – hindsight is a brilliant thing).

Following the visit, when we're back at school, we can get things moving by throwing in a wondering:

'Our visit to the gallery was great, wasn't it? I wonder what it would be like if we opened a gallery of our own here in school.'

We're fishing for a response here, but given the great time we had at the gallery looking at the naked people, we can almost guarantee that we'll get the show of interest and buzz that we're after. After agreeing that this would be a good thing to do, we can start to crank the engagement up by encouraging the children to imagine how it might happen:

> 'We'd have to find a space in school, wouldn't we? Somewhere nice and big ... Then we'd have to decide what we wanted the space to look like. The gallery we went to yesterday had different sections, didn't it? There was a cafe, a shop ... I wonder what makes a really great gallery?'

Now, before we get too carried away, we can't forget that the main point of this is to access that potentially dull but important learning about light. This is going to involve us pretty much deciding the nature of the exhibition, but even though we need to control this aspect, there'll still be the opportunity for the children to get involved in the decision-making further down the line.

> 'There's a lot to think about, and there'll be a lot to do. To help us, I've had an idea about the kind of work we could exhibit. Have a look at these pictures that I came across after our visit.'

In a 'here's one I prepared earlier' type move, we can now show the class a range of photographs that we've collected from various sources that show some brilliantly interesting and attention-grabbing effects – shadows, reflection, light spectrum, etc. (You'll find some great ones on the Internet – try an image search for the following keywords or phrases to get you started: 'Invisible girl with mirror', 'Nosferatu', 'Golden Gate raindrops'.)

Now we're really on track. All we've got to do is make sure we don't stuff things up by solely relying on the 'pupils should be taught' nonsense to reach our outcome. Instead of completely ignoring the direct teaching side of things, we can use it as and when it's needed. To make the most of this project, however, we've got to make sure that there's a healthy balance of creative learning opportunities for the children.

It may be that we start with some direct teaching. After all, the children might not have much – or any – experience with cameras other than some quick snaps with a smartphone. Maybe we could up the ante a bit and – to give a real sense of importance and authenticity to the project – bring in a local professional photographer to run a workshop with the children. They could teach them the basics, look at aspects of composition, or perhaps explore some of the great apps that can help amateur photographers look a bit more like they know what they're doing.

With the basic skills sorted thanks to a burst of direct teaching, we could move on to some of the science learning by adopting a 'teaching by not actually teaching them anything at all' approach. Using the same Guerrilla Guide to Creative Learning wheel as before, what would it look like if we sent children off to explore an aspect of light without bothering with the direct teaching bit?

Well, it would lead to chaos, but managing this potential disaster is exactly what the wheel is for, so have a look at the one shown here which I've completed with tips and ideas for this project.

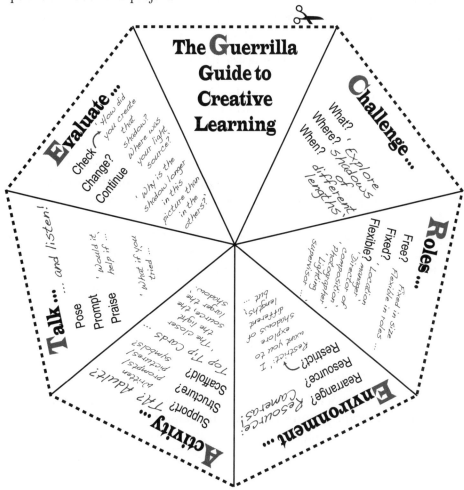

As you can see from the wheel, the challenge in the lesson is for the children to explore shadows of different lengths. In terms of roles, the sense of collective responsibility that the children will have for the opening of the gallery should lead to the perfect conditions to develop collaboration. Because children are children though, there's no getting away from the fact that if we put them in groups and leave them to their own devices, a bit like with the flower, they'll be scrapping before we know it. To avoid this, we could have dedicated roles, identified with name badges and explained to the children. Obviously, they all want to be the one who takes the photos, so our challenge is to create other roles that are equally important. Location manager, director of composition, photographer and lighting supervisor all fit the bill, and the children will know from the start that they will each get a turn at all of the roles in the group.

With the roles sorted, our next consideration is what to do with the environment. For lots of schools, one of the first decisions we'd need to make about resources could well be taken out of our hands. We may only be able to get hold of a limited number of cameras for the children to use. As a minimum, we'd need six, but even if you were very well resourced there'd be no point in providing too many as this would reduce the size of the groups and we'd lose the potential for collaboration. Another thing to think about is just what will happen when the children get their hands on the camera. If we send a group of four or five young people out and about in school to take photographs with a digital camera, I think there's only one likely outcome: hundreds of pictures, the majority of which will be blurred selfies. To avoid this, we can add another restriction, which will add an extra layer of challenge and also a healthy dose of tension. What if the group were sent out to explore shadows of different lengths, but were only allowed to take four photographs? The impact of this would be instant. If they're only allowed to take four photographs, then there's pressure to get things right. This would translate to the group members having to slow down and think much more carefully about what they were doing. Suddenly, the different roles in the group carry much more importance, and if we ensure that the number of photographs they're limited to matches the number of children in the group, everyone gets to try out all of the roles in turn.

This limitation is also a massive help when the children return to class. There'd be no point taking the pictures if we weren't going to look at them, and rather than having to wade through thousands of pretty average offerings, we'll have around thirty much higher quality photographs that the children will be proud to display.

Now that we've created the right conditions for the learning to happen, we can think about what kind of support, structure or scaffolding children might need when they're engaged in the activity. First of all, we might consider the children who we'd want to keep a special teacher eye on. You know the ones I mean, and there are always a couple who need a bit of extra supervision if you're to avoid the school being turned upside down. If there's a teaching assistant who could step into this role, then brilliant; but, if not, I'd be tempted to make the classroom into a photography studio for this group so I could help to manage them myself. Next, we'll need to think about how we might support or scaffold the learning, and we could intervene where necessary with some pre-prepared prompts that up to this point have been kept well hidden. It might be enough to give a verbal prompt to provide the children with the jumpstart they need, or it could come in the form of a sound-bitey top tip card that we whip out from our guerrilla utility belt:

'The closer the light source, the larger the shadow. Talk to each other about how that might help, and I'll come back in a few minutes to see how you're getting on.'

This could be enough, but in the unlikely event that the children are still confused and frustrated, then there's nothing wrong with stepping back into direct teacher mode for a minute and modelling an example for them:

'I tell you what. I'll show you how to set up the first photograph, and then you can do the rest.'

Now, with most eventualities covered, we can move on to the things that we do when things are going to plan … talk. We've already done a bit of prompting, but now's a good time to think about how to manage the groups that are getting a bit comfortable with the activity. What we need here are a couple of spanners to throw in the works to keep things interesting and – more importantly – to make them think.

'That's a really interesting photo. I wonder why the shadow is longer in that one than in the other pictures?'

'Why do you think shadows are the same shape as the object you used to create them? Does this always happen?'

'Could you take a photograph that has no shadow?'

And as soon as they're on to something, or they discover an interesting line of enquiry, then we'll use praise to keep things ticking along.

As I identified earlier, the real challenge here is not to talk, but to shut up. When children are engaged in a task, they're in the zone. Having some adult interjecting with bits of science language will be ignored, and so we're best to save our breath. We do want the children to know and use the correct language, but we need to have a bit of patience, our time will come.

The final section, Evaluate, sits at the back end of the wheel, but we've actually been doing this throughout the session. Using Check. Change? Continue has allowed us to keep children focused on exploring the areas we're interested in, but what about the learning?

Along with the questioning we've used during their group work, the best way to check what the children have been up to is to bring them back together to look at what they've done. Ideally, we'll be able to share their photos via the magic of technology on our interactive whiteboards or whatever equivalent you have. As we're only looking at a limited number of photographs, we can ask the children to take it in turns to come out and talk about their work. At this point we have a captive audience: rather than looking at some random images from the Internet, each group's work is now the focus of the lesson.

As the children are talking about their photographs, we can be checking the language that they're using. It would be a bit of a shock if they automatically started to use the correct scientific language – instead, it's much more likely that they'll still use their own words to explain what's going on. Having kept our mouths shut throughout, it's now time to stop withholding our expertise and start feeding in the language that we'd like them to use. The change is obviously important, and by wording this carefully, you can make sure that there's very good reason for it to happen:

'Let me just stop you for a minute … do you know what I've just realised? If we exhibit these photographs in our gallery, we'll have to explain how we composed them to any visitors that come. We might even have to produce some of those fancy guides that we saw on our trip. I suppose we'll have to make sure that we know what we're talking about, won't we? Let me give you some words that might help …'

While this might seem like a long-winded introduction to your direct teaching section, what we're aiming to do is reinforce the purpose and point of the lesson. The children aren't learning these words because they *have* to; they're learning them because they *need* to, and as soon as we've got children who desperately need to learn then we've well and truly cracked it.

The following lesson, whenever it happens, could follow the same structure. You might even keep the challenge the same, to allow the children to have a go at improving their first attempts. To increase ownership of the project, this could be a decision that the children make for themselves, along with choosing which aspect of light to investigate next.

As the sessions progress and the children's knowledge about light grows, there'll be plenty of other non-science-related opportunities for learning that can be added to the project. Thanks to our faulty connections switch, it's impossible not to start seeing the links to other areas of learning when you're planning a project like this. Along with being helpful, though, it can also be our worst enemy. It's incredibly easy to get carried away, and what was intended to be a six-week unit of work soon turns into an all-consuming three-year project.

We should definitely make sure there is some English work in there and, given the range of opportunities on offer, I'd be tempted to link several pieces of writing to the project. There'd be brochures to produce, invitations to write, and advertising and promotional work to be done. Along with English, there's also plenty of potential for maths. I'm sure I've seen a TV programme that showed people at a London gallery getting ready for an exhibition. There was a lot of measuring going on, and I think there's a rule for how high on a wall you should hang artworks, which depends on the average height of the people viewing it. If your gallery is being set up for parents, where should the class position their work? How could the children work it out? (There's a piece of homework in that that's actually worth doing for a change!) What about making this suitable for Year 1s?

Beyond this, you could take your pick. Maybe there's some history in there, or music that would complement the work (think scary shadow photos and creepy music!). The children could draw up the blueprints for the gallery layout in design technology – and perhaps even provide the hors-d'oeuvres for opening night!

Regardless of how many ideas we have, we need to know when to stop, and a few well-chosen connections is much better than a wheelbarrow full of dodgy ones. Being selective before we start also has the huge advantage of leaving some space for exploring new things that might crop up along the way.

The Reggio Emilia approach is a child centred model of early years education that was first developed in the Northern Italian city of the same name. As part of its many innovative practices, it uses the idea of something called 'emergent objectives'. I really like this thinking, and it's a great way of keeping an open mind – and an open ear – to the areas of the project that are really grabbing the children's attention. Being open to this, and also to the children's suggestions, allows us to feed their ideas into future sessions, and before long the potentially dull but important learning is a distant memory and the children's intrinsic motivation is sky-high.

In this chapter, I've looked at one particular project, but hopefully the potential and possibility of this approach stands out a mile.

If we were interested in mixing things up a bit (and increasing the risk a bit too), we can complement your projects with a more dramatic approach. When we looked at the sticks, and then also at the third CSI flower lesson, we began with a story. Stories have a powerful effect on us: they draw us in, keep us on the edge of our seats, and they're memorable. With the sticks, it was a very open-ended approach, which is exactly the way that foundation stage works. When we looked at addressing a specific area of the curriculum with the parts of the flower, things became more focused, and the direction of the story was largely shaped by the teacher. Having said this, the very fact that it is a story meant that the CSI tale could easily lead to a longer, more involved piece of work.

To make the most of this, and to help turn the ideas from our project into a story, we can use a brilliantly useful technique called 'Mantle of the Expert'. When I dealt with the sticky business of lying to children, I talked about a woman called Dorothy Heathcote. Along with bypassing the need to lie to children about learning, Dorothy also developed a system for using drama as a medium to access pretty much any area of the curriculum. She called this approach the 'Mantle of the Expert'. Before going any further, it's worth pointing out that I don't consider myself an expert at using this, and what follows is definitely a guerrilla take on it, rather than a true reflection of Dorothy's work.[3]

'Mantle of the Expert' involves children working on different areas of the curriculum as if they were experts. They could be engineers working on a construction project, explorers investigating a newly discovered island or maybe, in our case, an art and design company that has to prepare for an exhibition.

I suppose you could argue that this is not a million miles away from the project-based learning we've looked at already: the children took on the role of a group of people who were working on a big task, and the outcome was an exhibition. The big difference, though, is not in the outcome, but in the journey the children take to get there, and in 'Mantle of the Expert', it's the human element that sets it apart.

Let's have a look at how it might happen.

Building the story

To start things off, we could use the same strategy as before and take the children to a real gallery, because there's nothing better than a real experience to fire the imagination. This time, when we're back at school, we can start with a similar wondering, but with a subtle difference in language: 'That visit to the gallery was great, wasn't it? I wonder what it would be like if we opened a gallery of our own? What do you think it would look like?'

---

3 If you're interested in finding out more, it'd be well worth looking up some of the books and papers that Dorothy wrote. The Mantle of the Expert website has a great reading list to get you started. See www.mantleoftheexpert.com/about-moe/books/.

After taking a couple of suggestions, we can halt the flow of ideas to suggest a different way forward: 'I tell you what, instead of talking about it, why don't we draw it instead?'

With the children helping to move furniture to the sides of the room, quickly whip out our multipurpose roll of lining paper and prepare a large rectangle in the middle of the classroom. Using the children as makeshift paperweights, we'd ask them to gather around the outside of the shape, and then position ourselves as close to cross-legged as possible in the middle of the bottom edge.

With a black marker pen at the ready, we can get the children to create the outline of a large rectangle, and when the pen arrives back to us, draw some doors. While this is happening, we can talk to the children about what they're drawing and explain that the weird shapes added by their teacher will represent the entrance to the gallery.[4]

We'll go on to say that the gallery they've drawn will help us with a story that we're going to make up together; a story about an art gallery.

Remind the class about their visit to the gallery yesterday and the things that they saw; photos might help with this if they're suffering from goldfish memory. When the ideas start to come, we can slow things down for a minute by introducing an activity: 'I suppose we'd need some of those things in our gallery too, wouldn't we?' 'Why don't we add some of the features we remember to our picture?'

Then, on pieces of paper with felt tip pens, the children can work in pairs or small groups to create the inside of the gallery by drawing the features they either recall or have imagined.

When they've finished, they can be added to the paper to build the gallery. Through discussion, additional walls or partitions may be drawn until everyone's happy that we've got a plan for what the gallery could look like.

We might well end the session here, depending on how long it's taken or how involved the children got. If it does end, we'll need to make sure that the work is photographed from as many angles as possible to record it. The next step is

---

4   Dorothy Heathcote referred to this kind of start (using drawings or images) as 'iconic', a reference to Jerome Bruner's Theory of Development. There are lots of examples of this on the Mantle of the Expert website, including some fantastic lesson plans by Tim Taylor whose ideas were the inspiration behind the topic I'm describing. See: http://www.mantleoftheexpert.com/category/planning/.

where things get interesting because it's time to introduce some of the characters in the story and find out about the commission.

To keep things simple, you could have just one character delivering the challenge to the children. This could come via a phone call, a letter, email, or whichever form of communication you fancy. Again, rather than just being an add-on to the project-based learning option, the use of a character means that we have an ever-present source of regulation and potential further challenge. Things could be progressing very nicely with the work, but then the next barrier that the children will have to overcome will only be a quick email away.

If we want things to get a bit more complicated (which is no bad thing), then we could create the potential for additional tension by adding another character.

The commission

In our work, the commission will come from the gallery owner, an art-loving local businesswoman who – while being very successful in her own field – has no experience of opening or running a successful gallery. With the children gathered around, we can show them the piece of paper that will contain the text from the email: 'Our story is going to start today when we receive an email. Could we agree that this piece of paper is an email from the owner of the gallery?'

This is classic Heathcote language and allows us to pretty much use whatever we want to represent something in the story, while at the same time encouraging 'buy in'. You could do it with a blank piece of paper with 'email' written on top, and then make up the contents as you go along, or you could have something prepared in advance, as shown below.

Email: To the members of Art Solutions Ltd.

As a successful local businesswoman with an interest in art, I was recently persuaded to buy a large gallery in the centre of (insert your town name). To begin with, I was very excited about this and arranged a special opening event on (insert endpoint of topic!). Since then, however, things have gone from bad to worse. First of all, the artist who was going to exhibit his work has let me down, which means that there is no artwork to fill the gallery! On top of this, I haven't got time to set up the gallery properly because my other businesses will suffer. I really don't know what to do, and was hoping that – because of your expertise – you would be able to help.

Kind regards

Ms Sophie Franklyn

After reading the letter from the deliberately lovely sounding Sophie, we can use some of the same language to position the children to make a response: 'Do you think we could imagine that it was our job to help someone in this position?'

We could expand on this to explore the company name and what kind of work might be involved: 'I suppose the owner got in touch because we can provide exactly what she needs. We'll need to be able to produce the art, and organise the exhibition. What do you think we should do next? Perhaps we need to find out a bit more.'

We could slow things down again by introducing another activity, with the children collecting ideas and composing a reply. If we wanted to keep things rolling, scribe their ideas for them.

Whichever you go for, you'll end up with a response that will help you to gather some of the information you need. To reinforce the positive outlook on life that the kind of person who buys a gallery on a whim must possess, the response should be a bit vague (particularly when talking about what the exhibition might be about), teamed with a grateful – 'all will now be alright' – kind of attitude. The more light-hearted the tone the better, to be honest, as it will contrast nicely with the next character to enter the mix: the beleaguered gallery manager.

In passing, the owner will make a brief reference to the manager as someone the class should contact (number provided) before happily signing off with the confidence of someone who has had her problems solved.

To keep things interesting, the next phase could include a bit of teacher role play to break the pattern of emails. Roping in a teaching assistant, we can again ask the children to imagine: 'Can we agree that for the next few minutes, (insert your teaching assistant's name) will play the part of the gallery manager?'

And after the children have agreed, the phone call will take place.

Ring-ring, ring-ring.

(Seems a bit old fashioned, this – you could always go for a different ringtone if you fancied it, but to be honest, if you're aiming for that level of realism you've probably gone too far!)

'Hello, Redbridge Gallery' (*or whatever you're calling it!*)

'Could I speak to the manager please?'

'This is the manager speaking.'

'Hello, I'm calling from Art Solutions Ltd because we were contacted by Sophie Franklyn, who I believe is the owner.'

'Go on.' (*in a slightly suspicious tone!*)

'We've been asked to help with an exhibition on the (*give date*).'

'Have you, now? Well, I suppose that's all sorted then, isn't it? We'll just put on an exhibition and everything will be fine!'

To the children:

'Has anyone noticed that he sounds a bit annoyed? I wonder what that's about!' (*More classic Mantle language to make sure that the tone has been noticed!*)

'I suppose you know exactly what you're doing, do you?'

'Well, we are a team of experts and we have worked on projects like this before.'

'And I should just take your word for it, should I? I've got a reputation to uphold here! You can't just waltz into a gallery and stick things up on the wall – I bet you haven't even been told what the exhibition is about, have you?'

'No, we haven't had that information yet – could you tell us?'

'The artist who cancelled was a photographer. A world-famous photographer, I might add – and even if you were able to help, I doubt very much that your work would be of the same standard.'

'Thank you for that. Before going any further, I'd like to talk to my colleagues. Would it be alright if we rang you back?' *(Note the use of 'colleagues' – showing that we're all in this together!)*

'Yes, that's fine, you have your meeting; I've got plenty of things to be getting on with. Goodbye.'

After the phone call has finished, your teaching assistant can come out of role and return to join the class. (This might sound obvious, but the last thing you need is your TA going all 'method' on you and swanning around for the rest of the day in character.)

'Wow, that was unexpected, wasn't it? Did anyone notice that he didn't sound that confident that we could do the job?'

'I wonder how we could convince him?'

Again, there's a bit of fishing going on here, and what we're after is the suggestion that we could show the owner some of our work. There's the potential here for something that just wouldn't be possible if we hadn't used a story.

Creating a portfolio for the company is one of the generic tasks that you'll come across if you have a delve around on the Mantle of the Expert website, and it's a really useful technique to use if you're in the position of having to convince someone that you're able to do any given job. What it also allows us to do is rewind to a point in the story where the company were trained in a particular skill or activity which led them to become the expert in the present. (Sounds more complicated than it is!) If the company name has been left undecided, we could also use this technique to go back and ask children to create the name, logo, website, stationery or whatever else you want: 'Now, if we're going to put together some examples of our work, it would probably help us to go back in time to the point where the members of the company were first developing their skills. We know that the exhibition is about photography, so I suppose we should imagine a time when we were learning to use our cameras.'[5]

When we've got agreement from the class that this is OK, and we're happy that they understand the shift in the story, we can move on to the photography – which will, in time, allow us to get to grips with the learning about light.

As before, depending on how we want to play things, we could either run the training ourselves, or bring in a professional. Either way, by the end, they'll be ready to start building the company portfolio.

At this point (time permitting), it would be good to get them to photograph pretty much whatever they wanted. There could be a company meeting to ensure that we have a broad range of subjects, but there's no need to focus on the light and shadow business just yet. Having children explore something purposefully but without restriction doesn't happen that often in school, so when opportunities present themselves, they are definitely not to be missed.

When the children are happy with their portfolio of work, it's time to jump forward in the story to the present and get back in touch with the grumpy gallery manager. This time, instead of us taking the lead, maybe one of the children would be happy to make the phone call. To ease them into the role play, and to make sure they stand a chance of competing with your Oscar hopeful TA, decide as a company what we'd say to the manager on the phone. Depending on what the children want to do, we could invite the manager to view our portfolio, or offer to visit the gallery to take him through our work and convince him that we're up to the job.

With a meeting date set, it feels like a good time to pause the story with the children. You don't have to, but we have to go home at some point, and also we're likely to be in a position where the children want to keep going. This might sound a bit weird, given that we'd usually pounce on this kind of engagement, but that would be forgetting the *EastEnders* effect. Now, I'm not a big watcher of *EastEnders*, but I do know what those drum beats at the end mean, and you can guarantee that if you go back to the final thirty seconds of the show there'll be some kind of cliff-hanger to keep us dangling until the next episode. Breaking your story into 'episodes' will help you re-create exactly the same effect and leave

---

5 Adapted/pinched from a great lesson plan by Tim Taylor about a mountain rescue team http://www.
   mantleoftheexpert.com/planning/the-mountain-rescue-team.

the children desperate to know when the next session will begin. You can't beat a bit of anticipation.

When we pick up the story again, the portfolio containing the children's work will be given the once-over by the gallery manager (your TA again). This could be made into a bit of a nerve-wracking process, but ultimately if your TA goes off-piste and in the excitement decides to reject the company's hard work, we're stuffed, so have a quiet word with her beforehand to make sure she agrees with your script. Following this, we've got the opportunity for the manager to grudgingly praise our company on the standard of its presentation, then give us more information about the exhibition – which has the working title, 'Light and Dark'.

The individual lesson structure that we looked at using the Guerrilla Guide to Creative Learning wheel would fit seamlessly in here as a company activity, and the children will access the science learning without having to break from the story. As with the project, we'll be working within a time frame to produce the artwork for the exhibition opening, but – thanks to our two characters – there'll be plenty of opportunity to add additional challenges and demands along the way.

Here are a couple of ideas for some desirable hiccups that could easily be added as the story progresses.

Health and safety: The manager seems exactly the kind of character who'd be only too happy to remind us of our health and safety responsibilities: 'You can't put those there', 'That exit's got to be clear', 'Please tell me you've got an evacuation plan!' Could the company respond in time for the exhibition to open?

Unreasonable demands: The character of the owner could also provide you with plenty of complications as the story progresses. She could well start bombarding the company with ideas for the exhibition: 'Have you thought about catering because there must be catering', 'I know I'm being a pain, but is the music sorted? We can't have visitors walking around in silence!' 'We should definitely have a red carpet – there'll be some very important people there. I suppose you've already planned the VIP area, haven't you? Haven't you?!'

While the company might be able to cope, it could all get a bit too much for the gallery manager, who might well throw in the towel. Would the company be able to save the day, or would they have a different response to this breakdown in relationships? (One group of militant youngsters in my class felt sorry for the overworked and undervalued manager, and decided to go on strike until the owner apologised and the manager was reinstated to his post.)

For me, putting together learning like this is one of the best bits about being a teacher. I mentioned *EastEnders* earlier, and writing all this down makes me feel like I'm preparing for some kind of soap opera or TV drama. I suppose that's not a bad way of thinking about it, and as long as we're leaving plenty of space for the children to make key decisions and shape the storyline alongside us, we won't go far wrong!

Being open to ideas in this way allows for the real moments of magic to happen – moments when the next move in the story is triggered by some unexpected gem of creativity from the children. They'll think of things that we would never have considered, and react in ways that we couldn't possibly predict. Whether we go for the project or the story, what we've achieved at the end is balance. We've got really strong elements of discovery and exploration, while at the same time we're delivering the direct teaching at just the right moments and for exactly the right reasons.

It almost goes without saying that this approach would work equally well in other areas of the curriculum. Covering subject knowledge is the easy part, but creating opportunities for children to explore what it means to be human is what really counts. Whether it's geography, history, DT or anything else we're doing, there's a story to be told or a project to be hatched in every topic we teach.

Chapter 15

WE ARE GUERRILLAS

At the start of the book, we looked at the kind of skills that we wanted our young people to develop.

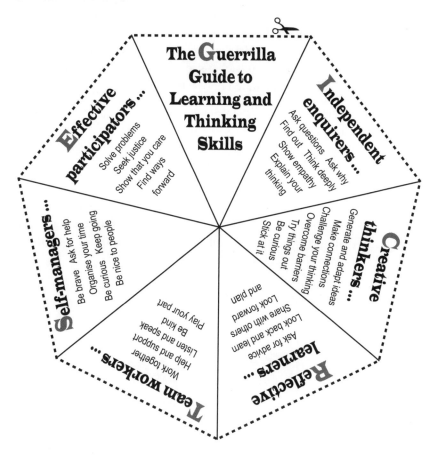

Creative thinking has been the driver for everything that's contained in this book – from nailing our teacher persona, up through the first floor of guerrilla HQ to the dizzy heights of the rooftop terrace. We've had the chance to model it, live and breathe it, and we've given our children the chance to develop it too.

A quick glance around the rest of the wheel only reinforces in my mind that this is definitely the way to go. From kangaroo testicles to gallery openings and everything in between, it's hard to see a single area of the wheel that hasn't been covered by the mix of skills, techniques and strategies that make up a guerrilla teacher.

And it's these tactics that this book is really about. Not the flowers or the sticks or the photography – because they're just ideas, the things that we hang it all on. It was never supposed to be about dishing up the finished article or providing ready-made lessons on a plate. I hope that this book provides food for thought. You could take the thinking behind the crime scene, the sticks, or the topic on light and apply it to anything, and that's exactly what you should do. And anyway, your ideas could well be much better than mine.

Ultimately, no two guerrillas will be the same, and it's not my job to tell you how to teach – just as it's not anyone else's. Being a guerrilla teacher is about being prepared, being creative and being adaptable, but most of all it's about standing up and doing what we believe to be right for our children.

This is why we shouldn't waste our time listening to a lot of the people who have something to say about education because, for all the time they spend nowhere near a classroom telling us how we should be one thing or the other, there'll be teachers like us using a whole range of different tactics and blending them together into a stunningly effective mix.

So put the book down, guerrilla, and stand to attention, because we're the people on the ground and we're about to change the world.

BIBLIOGRAPHY

Beadle, P. (2015) *Literacy: Commas, Colons, Connectives and Conjunctions.* Carmarthen: Crown House Publishing.

Bjork, E.L. and Bjork, R.A. (2011) Making things hard on yourself, but in a good way: Creating desirable difficulties to enhance learning. In M.A. Gernsbacher, R.W. Pew, L.M. Hough and J.R. Pomerantz (eds), *Psychology and the Real World: Essays illustrating fundamental contributions to society.* New York: Worth Publishers.

Bjork, R.A. (2013) Desirable difficulties perspective on learning. In H. Pashler (ed.), *Encyclopedia of the Mind.* Thousand Oaks, CA: Sage Reference.

Brunton, P. and Thornton, L. (2010) *Bringing the Reggio Approach to your Early Years Practice.* Oxon: Routledge.

Clarke, A.C. (1979) *The View from Serendip.* London: Macmillan.

Claxton, G. (2006) *Learning to Learn – The Fourth Generation.* Bristol: TLO Limited.

Curran, A. (2008) *The Little Book of Big Stuff About the Brain.* Carmarthen: Crown House Publishing.

de Bono, E. (1993) *Sur/petition: Going Beyond Competition.* London: HarperCollins.

Department for Education (2013) *National Curriculum in England Key Stages 1 and 2 Framework Document.* London: DFE. Available at: https://www.gov.uk/government/uploads/system/uploads/attachment_data/file/425601/PRIMARY_national_curriculum.pdf.

Edmiston, B. and Taylor, T. (2015) The Mountain Rescue Team. Available at: http://www.mantleoftheexpert.com/planning/the-mountain-rescue-team/.

Gilbert, I. (2002) *Essential Motivation in the Classroom.* Oxon: Routledge Falmer.

Hattie, J. and Yates, G. (2014) *Visible Learning and the Science of How We Learn.* Oxon: Routledge.

Heathcote, D. (1984) *Collected Writings on Education and Drama.* London: Hutchinson & Co. Ltd.

Mantle of the Expert website. http://www.mantleoftheexpert.com.

McLeod, S. (2012) *Bruner*. Available at: http://www.simplypsychology.org/bruner.html.

National Advisory Committee on Creative and Cultural Education (NACCCE) (1999) All Our Futures: Creativity, Culture and Education. London: DFEE.

Qualifications and Curriculum Authority (2011) *A framework of personal learning and thinking skills*. London: DFE. Available at: http://webarchive.nationalarchives. gov.uk/20110223175304/http:/curriculum.qcda.gov.uk/key-stages-3-and-4/skills/personal-learning-and-thinking-skills/index.aspx.

Robinson, K. (2001) *Out of Our Minds: Learning to be Creative*. West Sussex: Capstone Publishing Limited.

Rogers, B. (2006) *Classroom Behaviour*. London: Paul Chapman Publishing.

Rose, Sir J. (2009) *Independent Review of the Primary Curriculum*. Nottingham: DCSF Publications. Available at: http://www.educationengland.org.uk/documents/pdfs/2009-IRPC-final-report.pdf.

Taylor, T. (2014) Why telling the truth is better for learning. Imaginative-inquiry, 28 August 2014. Available at: http://www.imaginative-inquiry.co.uk/2014/08/why-telling-the-truth-is-better-for-learning/.

Taylor, T. The Victorian Workhouse Museum (n.d.). Available at: http://www.mantleoftheexpert.com/planning/victorian-workhouse-museum/.

Tiley-Nunn, N. (2014) *Primary Maths*. Carmarthen: Crown House Publishing.

Wagner, B.J. (1976) *Dorothy Heathcote: Drama as a Learning Medium*. Cheltenham: Hutchinson Education.

INDEX

Index of strategies

978-1-78135-236-6

Ian Gilbert

with Mark Anderson, Lisa Jane Ashes, Phil Beadle, Jackie Beere, David Cameron (The Real David Cameron), Paul Clarke, Tait Coles, Mark Creasy, Mark Finnis, Dave Harris, Crista Hazell, Martin Illingworth, Nina Jackson, Rachel Jones, Gill Kelly, Debra Kidd, Jonathan Lear, Trisha Lee, Roy Leighton, Matthew McFall, Sarah Pavey, Simon Pridham, Jim Roberson, Hywel Roberts, Martin Robinson, Bethan Stracy-Burbridge, Dave Whitaker and Phil Wood.

www.independentthinkingpress.com